the really, truly, honest-to-goodness

ONE-POT COOKBOOK

by **Jesse Ziff Cool**

photographs by **David Prince**

CHRONICLE BOOKS

SAN FRANCISCO

Library of Congress Cataloging-in-Publication Data available.

ISBN-13: 978-0-8118-4500-7
ISBN-10: 0-8118-4500-1

Manufactured in China.

Prop styling by **Cindy di Prima**
Food styling by **Michael Pederson**
Designed by **Brooke Johnson**
Typesetting by **Janis Reed**

Distributed in Canada by Raincoast Books
9050 Shaughnessy Street
Vancouver, British Columbia V6P 6E5

10 9 8 7 6 5 4 3 2 1

Chronicle Books LLC
85 Second Street
San Francisco, California 94105

www.chroniclebooks.com

ACKNOWLEDGMENTS

This book is dedicated to the memory of my father, Eddie Ziff. Dad was an infamous character, selling produce for thirteen years at both the Menlo Park and Palo Alto Farmers' Markets. He naturally took whatever was in season, put it in a pot, stirred, tasted, seasoned, and created delicious one-pot dishes that are now an important part of my everyday cooking.

My mom, June, is the most loving mother on the planet and has the most experience with my one-pot experiments. Her simple yet discriminating palate sampled from the many plastic containers full of one-pot wonders that ended up in her refrigerator. She was honest about how they tasted, gently giving me suggestions on ways to improve. In every way, she remains genuinely supporting of who I am: a gift beyond price.

Thank you my patient, supportive family: especially my sons, Jonah and Joshua, and Joshua's beautiful family, Yuko, Masa, and Miya. We all realize that one-pot cooking is a natural and loving way of preparing food, always in my kitchen and now their own. Thanks Eric for being my friend and sharing one-pot meals, possibly more often than any other, and always with vigor.

For me to cook up a book in the midst of running three restaurants and an ever-growing catering company means lots of support from my remarkable staff. Thank you Kendra Tidwell and Don Boyles for their great leadership. I especially want to thank Francisco Medrano for so many years of watching over Flea St. Café with love and care.

Thank you Sandra Heuckroth for testing recipes.

Thank you for looking over the manuscript, my dear friend Meesha Halm. Your keen eye and love of food is always valued and important to me.

Amy Treadwell and Bill LeBlond at Chronicle Books remain open to new ideas. It is a pleasure to work with them.

When I first saw the photographs for this book, they actually made me hungry. Thank you David Prince.

contents

INTRODUCTION

Nothing is more inviting than a pot of something wonderful simmering on the stove, the intoxicating scents filling the air with home-cooked warmth. Who can resist a mouthwatering seafood stew, a cut-with-a-spoon braised lamb shank, or falling-off-the-bone ribs? For three decades now, one of my favorite ways of nurturing people at my restaurants has been this style of Old World rustic comfort food.

But as someone who works a lot and yet still likes to eat at home, I know how difficult it is to walk through the front door after a long day of work and prepare a meal from scratch—not to mention the part of a meal we often forget: the time needed to clean up from the beginning to the end of the process.

This book is about one-pot cooking, my favorite way to prepare meals. The question often arises: Is it possible to cook everything in one pot without sacrificing the quality or integrity of ingredients? As I hope to show you in this book, the answer is a hearty yes.

In the past few years, I've rediscovered the gratification and ease of preparing soul-satisfying dishes that use common ingredients and are cooked in one vessel, be it a pot, skillet, steamer, Dutch oven, or my beloved slow cooker. Simmered stews, braises, quick sautés, pastas, casseroles, and even a meat loaf cooked on the stove top are always welcome around my house. Cooking for others is one of the most nurturing gifts we can give, and the beauty of these dishes is that they simplify mealtime.

Cooking in one vessel is nothing new. From the earthenware tagines of Morocco and shabu-shabu cauldrons of Japan to the woks of China and the simmering vats of curries of India, one-pot cooking has culinary footprints all around the world. Many dishes were inspired by necessity when hard times called for humble ingredients and less-expensive cuts of meat. Those foods, their flavors most often summoned through long, moist cooking methods, are the ones that come to mind when we think of home-cooked meals. Others were born of religious reasons. Orthodox Jews, who were forbidden to work on the Sabbath, prepared rich, savory one-pot stews before sundown, and then left them to simmer until sunrise, when the fast was broken.

As I was growing up, this was often the way my grandmother cooked. Some of my earliest memories of Nana are of her standing at the stove stirring a giant batch of tomato sauce or a traditional Italian creamed salt cod. There was always something simmering there on her back burner. I have no memories of her ever using a grill or the broiler. She even browned the bread we used for sopping in the pot to absorb every last bit of juice or food. She cooked most everything in a cast-iron skillet or in a large, heavy pot with a chipped enamel lid. While I'll never forget that old pot, which is now long gone, it was never really about the pot. It was more about the allure of discovering and tasting what was inside that mattered to me.

My love of one-pot cooking continued when I was a college student, living in married housing at Western Michigan University. I was surrounded by families from everywhere on the planet, and everyone knew that I was curious about more than just American styles of cooking. A Nigerian woman always had a pot of something wonderful simmering on her back burner. She frequently invited me to her home to taste her spicy concoctions. It was there I was inspired by the endless possibilities of cooking in one vessel, far beyond my Nana's personal cuisine.

To that pot, the Nigerian woman added whatever she had brought home from the market that day. For me, it was a learning experience in how to cook with seasonal ingredients. A few times a week, I knocked on her door like a beggar, hoping for a small sample from her nearly addictive cauldron.

THE ART OF ONE-POT MEALS

The rich tradition of one-pot cooking has inspired this collection of recipes, which include bone-sticking comfort foods as well as elegant do-ahead entrées that make entertaining a snap. These dishes are no less sensuous or satisfying than what I would serve at my restaurants. In fact, a good handful come from recipes used at Flea Street Café, my white-tablecloth restaurant in Menlo Park, California.

I've modified and simplified many of these dishes to create delicious complete meals. You will discover how it can indeed all be done in one vessel.

After all, the premise of one-pot cooking is that it should be efficient. At times, with recipes such as a curry, the list of ingredients might be long, but the preparation is not complicated. In others, the list is brief, but the process takes a bit more time, especially when you are first learning how to cook in stages in one pot.

An honest-to-goodness one-pot dish is one in which all the ingredients (except for garnishes) are at some point either cooked or reheated in one pot, whether slowly or quickly. This book is all about that pot and how the flavor of each ingredient develops and melds with those of the other ingredients.

This doesn't mean that everything is always just dumped into a pot, though sometimes it is. And this is not just a book about stews and soups, though food ladled from a pot can be a wonderful respite from *à la minute*, overly designed haute cuisine.

In one-pot cooking, some basic techniques should be followed to ensure the best texture, flavor, and eye appeal. Browning meat, poultry, or fish and then adding ingredients in descending order of cooking times will produce a delicious and attractive one-pot dish (see the "Tips and Techniques" chapter).

SOUPS, STEWS, AND BEYOND

One-pot cooking naturally lends itself to rustic stews and braises that simmer on low heat for hours. For the modern cook, these slow-cooked foods can be a godsend, since they can be assembled and left on the stove while life goes on.

Many of these dishes taste even better a day or two later and can be reheated again and again without compromising their quality. When I cook at home, I plan on having leftovers. In the back of my mind, often because, like others, I am harried, many one-pot recipes are designed to be served for more than just one meal. For families where dinner often has to be reheated several times to accommodate soccer practice, FedEx deadlines, and other mealtime interruptions, consider which recipe might be doubled to fit into your weekly meal planning.

You can also freeze, or better yet, vacuum pack the leftover part of the dish. Imagine rewarding yourself later with a nutritious, delicious home-cooked meal at your fingertips.

Don't think that one-pot cooking is only heavy, cold-weather food. Many of the recipes are for seasonal fare, such as quick, light stews, sautés, and summery casseroles prepared in a skillet. Turn to these recipes after a long day of outdoor play, or a spontaneous trip to the farmers' market, or on a warm evening when you're hungry but in the mood for something that you can prepare quickly, in one pot.

ON THE SIDE

Most of the recipes in this book provide a complete meal when served with a green salad or a piece of crusty, warm bread to sop up their rich and delicious juices. But if a dish doesn't include a starch, a protein, or a vegetable, you can opt for your own choice. Add meat or fish to a vegetarian dish, or rice or pasta to an all-vegetable or all-meat recipe. Almost any dish benefits from a handful of seasonal vegetables being tossed into the pot just in time to cook them to perfection.

A steamer basket is invaluable for reheating precooked components of a one-pot dish. I have a few different sizes that fit inside my favorite pots. The steam from whatever is cooking in a pot is intense. Not only can it warm foods, it can also cook an ingredient from scratch if you prefer not to place it directly in the cooking liquid.

FROM THE POT TO THE TABLE

Don't be afraid to serve your dish straight from the pot, especially when the pot is a beautiful one. There are great-looking cast-iron, ceramic, and enamel-coated casseroles that can double as both a pot and a serving dish.

For me, nothing is more nurturing than dining family style from one vessel, with everyone ladling out big bowls of food that has cooked for hours. This kind of ritual can be either rustic or elegant, depending on how you set the table.

Accompanied with beautiful linens and flatware, a gorgeous pot can show off in center stage. Grab your favorite pot holders, crumple a beautiful dish towel in the middle of the table or set a trivet there, and place the pot right on top.

A big beautiful platter or serving bowl is an elegant way to present a meal, whether standing alone or nestled next to complementary side dishes. And don't forget how a final garnish of herbs, cheese, or green onions can enhance both the beauty and flavor of your one-pot wonder.

MAKE IT EASY

Nonstick pots have a place in one-pot cooking, especially when they are high in quality. There are a handful of dishes in this book that are served unmolded. A nonstick pot or skillet makes that part of the process a lot easier. A nonstick surface is not the best choice for dishes in which the meat or poultry is browned first, however, as the flavorful browned juices that season braised dishes will not coat a nonstick surface.

This book is meant to open your mind to the endless possibilities of one-pot cooking. Once you've embraced some basic techniques, which mostly involve timing, you'll be able to use the recipes simply as a road map. As with any cookbook, the recipes can be tailored to suit your own tastes and lifestyle.

One final thought: An underappreciated bonus of one-pot cooking is the minimal cleanup involved. That, for me, is often the best part of all. (Well, besides the leftovers!)

TIPS and Techniques

EQUIPMENT

Choosing the Right Pot

One-pot meals can be prepared in a variety of cooking vessels, including earthenware tagines; clay pots and slow cookers; rice and pressure cookers; stock- and pasta pots; cast-iron and enamelware Dutch ovens; and stainless-steel, cast-iron, or anodized aluminum skillets.

To succeed at one-pot cooking, you don't have to run out and purchase any special pots. Unless otherwise specified, all that is required are a few good, heavy pots of varying sizes with tight-fitting lids. You can cook everything in this book in one of three pots: an 8-quart pasta pot with strainer and steamer inserts, an 8-quart soup pot or Dutch oven, or a heavy 12-inch skillet.

If you don't have the right-sized pot, in most cases, err in using a larger one. Food cooks better and more evenly when there is more space in the pot.

If you use a specialty pot, such as a slow cooker or a pressure cooker, the cooking time will vary accordingly, so be sure to check the manufacturer's manual. If the recipe calls for browning, you can opt to skip that step or brown the food in a skillet before proceeding with the recipe.

Other Utensils

Besides your pots, I suggest you have on hand an instant-read thermometer, restaurant-quality tongs, a slotted metal spatula, a long, sturdy fork to remove large ingredients as you cook in stages, a slotted spoon, and a ladle.

THE GOLDEN RULES OF ONE-POT COOKING

While the possibilities for one-pot meals are endless, there are a few techniques that should be followed to ensure the best texture, flavor, and eye appeal.

Timing

The main rule for one-pot cooking is to add the ingredients in order of their cooking time, from dense or dry foods that take a long time to cook to those that cook quickly and so should be added at the very end, to just heat through before serving. Bear this in mind when making seasonal substitutions. Add sturdy, long-cooking vegetables such as root vegetables and winter squash early, and delicate, quick-cooking ingredients, such as peas, corn, or delicate greens, toward the end.

Do Ahead

Streamline your mealtime by preparing vegetables and other ingredients in advance. Set them aside to add to the pot at the correct time in order to cook them to the desired doneness.

Browning

Although this step is not absolutely necessary, most of the time I brown meat, poultry, or fish first. I then remove it with tongs or a slotted spoon, returning it to the pot to finish cooking later. Browning, or searing food on all sides over high heat, accomplishes several things.

First, it gives food a nice appearance, which can't be achieved by simply poaching it in the pot. Browning also caramelizes the natural sugars in the food, imparting a nutty flavor. The brown bits and juices released from the browning will meld with the other flavors of the pan sauce.

You don't need to pour off all the fat that remains in the pot after browning meat, poultry, or fish. Instead, some of that fat is used to cook the remaining ingredients. I can't think of a better way to build layers of flavor.

When browning leaner cuts of meat, such as loin or tender chops, and foods that cook quickly, take care not to overcook them, or your finished dish will be tough.

Choose Seasonal Ingredients

To get the optimum flavor in any dish, start with locally grown seasonal ingredients. Use fresh organic foods whenever possible. Go to farmers' markets and specialty produce stores for vegetables and fruits, or start a small garden. When fresh is not available, consider using frozen or dried alternatives, such as tomatoes, corn, peas, and even beans. This is the key to good cooking. When winters are long, the use of locally preserved foods imparts many of the same delicious flavors.

Stock or Broth

Stock or broth is often the foundation of a one-pot meal. Making your own stock is great, but it's perfectly acceptable to use a canned or boxed low-sodium broth (organic when possible) when the recipes in this book call for broth. If you do make your own stock, double the recipe and freeze half of it in resealable plastic bags or ice cube trays to use later.

Doneness

Tune in to how a dish looks, smells, and tastes to judge when it's perfectly cooked. Enjoy the aromas and allow them to inform you of the progress of your dish. Along with smelling and looking at your one-pot meal as it cooks, don't forget to take periodic tastes. Follow the directions in each individual recipe as a general guideline to check for doneness. But above all, trust your senses.

ONE-POT MEALS

The majority of the dishes in this book may be served as a complete meal. One-pot recipes that don't contain a protein, vegetable, or starch can be served with side dishes, but this being *The Really, Truly, Honest-to-Goodness One-Pot Cookbook*, I've come up with a handful of creative ways to prepare these accompaniments in the same pot.

Pastas and Whole Grains

One way to enrich a soupy, saucy one-pot dish is to thicken it with pasta or grains. You can approach this from two directions. One way is to cook the pasta or grain ahead of time in the pot, remove it, and set it aside, keeping it warm or at least at room temperature. Grains can be reheated later by steaming them briefly in an insert set into your pot. The second way is to add pastas or grains directly to the pot.

Dried pasta or quick-cooking rice can be added to juicy creations toward the end of the cooking process, following the directions on the package. If necessary, add a bit more liquid to the pot to cook your grain properly.

Some quick-cooking grains and pastas, such as couscous, bulgur (cracked wheat), kasha, or amaranth, need to be cooked in the pot for only 5 minutes or so.

Remember, however, the starch from an added grain or pasta will become a part of the dish, thickening and possibly clouding the juices.

Potatoes, Polenta, and Stuffings

Some dishes cry out to be ladled over a mound of mashed potatoes, creamy polenta, or homemade stuffing. In these cases, I recommend that you cook these side dishes ahead of time, and then reheat them in a bowl or casserole that fits into a steamer basket inserted in the pot during the last 5 minutes or so of the cooking process. In the case of stuffed pork chops, the stuffing is cooked right on top of the dish. If the mashed potatoes or polenta have been made in the pot ahead of time and then removed, reheating in the microwave might be the perfect solution.

Vegetable Sides

Quick-cooking vegetables, such as peas, beans, asparagus, chard, and florets of cauliflower or broccoli, can be cooked in a steamer insert or basket inserted in the pot. To add more flavor, toss vegetables with spices or a few sprigs of herbs or slices of citrus before steaming them. The cooking time of a vegetable is determined by its density and the desired degree of doneness. Figure out how long the vegetable would take to cook on its own and add it to the pot accordingly.

PRESENTATION

I like to serve food family style, on platters, in big bowls, or in an attractive pot so people can serve themselves. Use large serving forks and spoons to serve your one-pot dish. Consider using cloth napkins in colorful patterns or earthy solids to offer more depth and appeal to your table. A good bottle of wine and a vase of fresh flowers are the perfect final touches.

FOLLOWING A RECIPE

I write cookbooks, and I want the recipes to work. But I know there are a myriad of factors that can make a recipe work or not. Fruits and vegetables vary in freshness, ripeness, flavor, water content, and sugar content. Meat, fish, and poultry differ too, and thus doneness can be longer or shorter than indicated.

So, I invite you to really cook with this book. Follow the recipes, but taste, taste, taste, and use aroma as a guide to add a little more of this or that, or to cook your dish a little less or a little longer. Start tasting before the indicated time of doneness in the recipe. Don't be afraid to add more salt, sugar, wine, or herbs, according to your own palate.

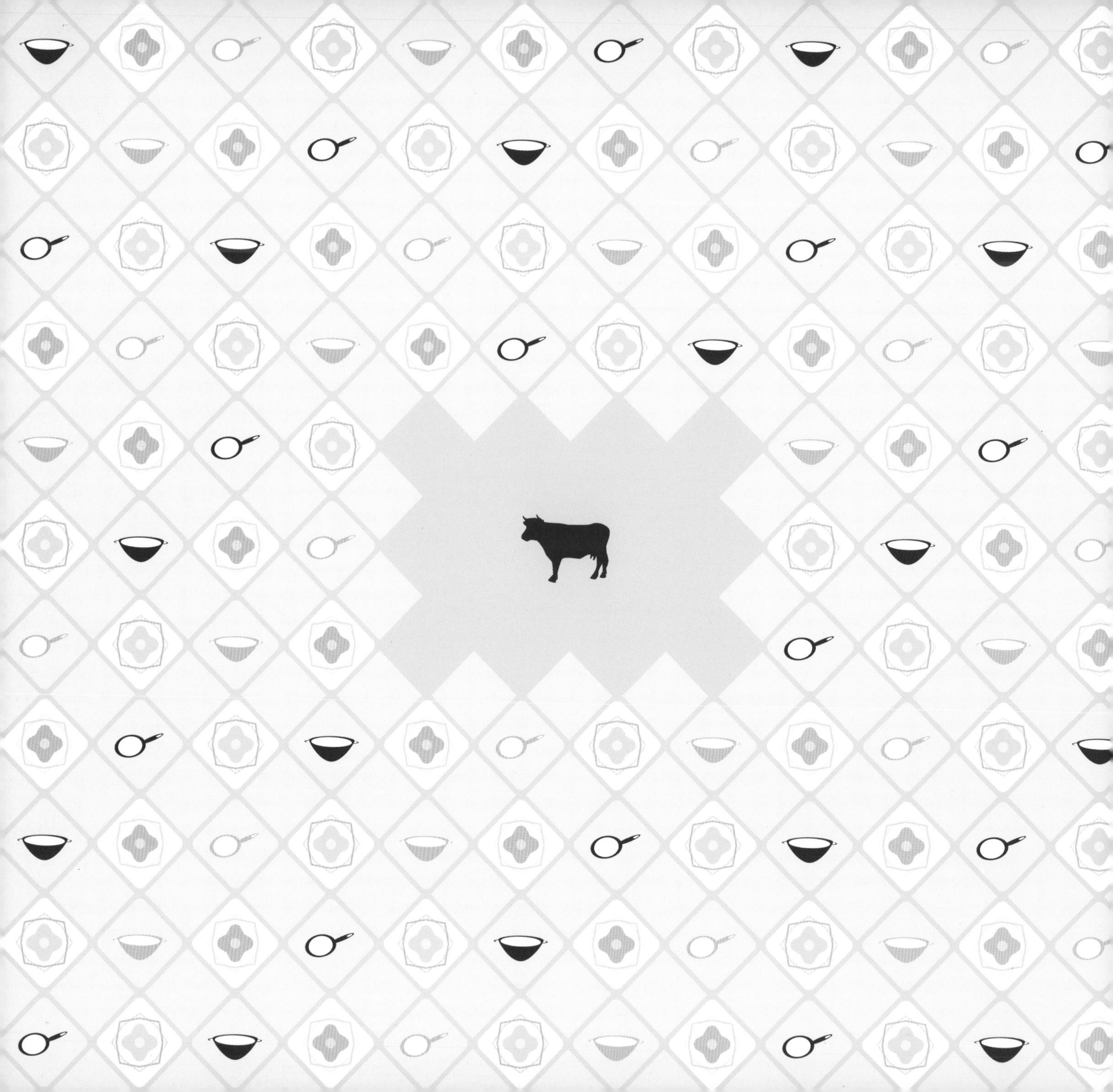

BEEF

Barbecued Carne asada with avocado-jicama Relish

Carne asada is a traditional Mexican dish of marinated and grilled meat used to fill tacos and burritos. In this one-pot adaptation, I cook the meat in a spicy homemade barbecue sauce to get the same zesty results. Slather the carne asada onto warm tortillas and top with the cooling avocado-jicama relish.

serving suggestion: Serve leftovers for breakfast, scrambled with eggs, or in crusty buns for barbecued beef sandwiches.

carne asada
2 pounds carne asada beef (thinly sliced
   top round, skirt, flank, or flap steak)
Salt and freshly ground pepper to taste
3 tablespoons olive oil

barbecue sauce
1 tablespoon chili powder
1 tablespoon sweet paprika
1 teaspoon mustard seeds

1 teaspoon ground cumin
1 yellow onion, finely chopped
2 cloves garlic, minced
One 8-ounce can tomato paste
2 very ripe tomatoes, seeded and chopped,
   or one 14-ounce can chopped tomatoes
1/3 cup packed brown sugar
1/2 cup red wine vinegar
2 tablespoons molasses
1 cup fresh orange juice

avocado-jicama Relish
1 large ripe avocado, peeled, pitted,
   and coarsely chopped
1 cup jicama, peeled and finely chopped
1 green onion, including green parts,
   finely chopped
Juice of 1 lime
Salt and freshly ground pepper to taste

12 warm flour or corn tortillas
Sour cream for garnish

SERVES 4 TO 6

Generously season the meat all over with salt and pepper. In a large, heavy pot, heat the olive oil over medium-high heat and cook the meat until browned, about 5 minutes on each side. Using tongs, transfer to a large cutting board.

To make the barbecue sauce: In the same pot, stir the chili powder, paprika, mustard seeds, and cumin over medium-high heat for 2 minutes, or until fragrant. Stir in the onion, garlic, tomato paste, and tomatoes. Cover, reduce heat to medium-low, and cook for about 10 minutes, or until the onion is soft. Add

>> >> >> >>

the brown sugar, vinegar, molasses, and orange juice. Reduce the heat to low and simmer uncovered, stirring occasionally, for 30 minutes, or until slightly thickened.

Meanwhile, make the relish: In a medium bowl, combine all the ingredients. Cover and refrigerate.

Just before serving, cut the beef against the grain, on the diagonal, into ½-inch-thick strips. Add to the pot and cook for about 5 minutes, or until the meat is warmed through.

Serve in the pot or in a deep platter, with the relish, tortillas, and sour cream alongside.

ULTIMATE LEFTOVERS:
STEAK AND SWEET POTATO HASH

One way I simplify mealtimes is to cook some extra food for dinner that can be incorporated into a breakfast dish the following day. The next time you find yourself barbecuing steaks for dinner, throw an extra steak on the grill. While you're at it, toss a couple of sweet potatoes in the oven, and you'll have all the makings for this quick and easy breakfast hash.

VARIATIONS: If you like eggs with your hash, just before serving, crack 4 to 8 eggs directly onto the hash, cover, and cook the eggs for 8 to 10 minutes or until cooked to the desired doneness. Or, remove the hash once it's done and scramble or fry the eggs directly in a little butter or oil in the pot.

3 tablespoons vegetable oil, plus more
   as needed
1 small onion, coarsely chopped
½ red bell pepper, seeded and coarsely
   chopped
1 cooked sweet potato or yam, peeled
   and cut into ½-inch dice

About 1 pound rib eye, New York, or
   strip steak, cooked rare and cut into
   ½-inch dice
1 teaspoon sweet paprika
4 tablespoons coarsely chopped fresh
   flat-leaf parsley
Salt and freshly ground pepper
   to taste

SERVES 4

In a medium or large heavy skillet, heat 3 tablespoons of oil over medium heat. Add the onion, bell pepper, and sweet potato and cook for 10 minutes, stirring occasionally, until the sweet potato begins to brown. Add the beef, paprika, 3 tablespoons of the parsley, and the salt and pepper.

Increase the heat to high and cook the hash, turning occasionally, until browned, about 5 minutes. To serve, use a metal spatula to transfer the hash to a large platter or warmed plates and garnish with the remaining 1 tablespoon of parsley.

CHATEAUBRIAND WITH MUSHROOMS AND LEEKS

This tender cut of beef from the center of the tenderloin is often served with a béarnaise sauce, but here I smother the roast in an unctuous leek and mushroom sauce. Chanterelles and other wild mushrooms lend an exquisite, earthy flavor to the dish, but any type of mushroom works well in this recipe.

VARIATIONS: For a complete meal, add diced potatoes or parsnips and an extra ½ cup broth along with the mushrooms. Or, add already cooked noodles to the sauce just before serving.

One 2-pound chateaubriand steak
Salt and freshly ground pepper to taste
2 tablespoons olive oil
2 tablespoons unsalted butter

3 cloves garlic, minced
2 large leeks, white parts only, washed and thinly sliced
8 ounces mushrooms, coarsely chopped

⅓ cup cream sherry
1 tablespoon minced fresh thyme
1 tablespoon minced fresh flat-leaf parsley
1 cup beef broth, plus more as needed

SERVES 4

Generously season the meat with salt and pepper. In a medium, heavy pot, heat the olive oil over medium-high heat and brown the roast for about 5 minutes on each side. Using tongs, transfer the steak to a large platter.

In the same pot, melt the butter over medium-low heat. Add the garlic and leeks and cook for 5 minutes, or until translucent. Add the mushrooms, sherry, thyme, parsley, and the 1 cup beef broth and season with salt and pepper to taste. Simmer for 10 minutes.

Return the steak to the pot and spoon the pan juices and mushrooms over it. Add more broth to the pot, if necessary, so that about one-third of the meat is submerged. Simmer, uncovered, turning occasionally, for about 45 minutes, or until an instant-read thermometer inserted in the center of the steak registers 130°F for medium-rare.

Transfer the steak to a cutting board and let rest for 5 minutes. Cut crosswise into ½-inch-thick diagonal slices.

To serve, arrange the sliced meat on a large warmed platter or individual plates and smother it with the mushroom sauce.

BRAISED CHUCK ROAST WITH BEETS AND PARSNIPS

Chuck roast, which comes from the shoulder and neck of the cow, is an extremely flavorful and economical cut of meat. Because it tends to be fibrous and has plenty of fat, it's a perfect candidate for braising slowly until the meat is meltingly tender and absorbs all the other flavors. The addition of semisweet chocolate and ruby port lends wonderfully complex layers of taste to the sauce. This recipe yields leftovers, because both the meat and sauce taste even better the next day.

SERVING SUGGESTION: The rich sauce in this dish is delicious served over mashed potatoes or cooked whole grains such as wheat berries or barley.

One 4-pound bone-in chuck roast
Salt and freshly ground pepper to taste
2 tablespoons olive oil
4 beets, peeled and cut into ½-inch wedges
2 parsnips, peeled and cut into ½-inch wedges

1 onion, cut into ½-inch wedges
2 stalks celery, cut into ¼-inch-thick slices
6 cloves garlic, minced
1 bay leaf
2 tablespoons minced fresh rosemary
1½ cups ruby port

2 ounces semisweet dark chocolate, grated
About 4 cups beef or chicken broth
2 tablespoons minced fresh flat-leaf parsley for garnish

SERVES 6

Generously season the meat with salt and pepper. In a large, heavy pot, heat the olive oil over medium-high heat and cook the chuck roast for about 20 to 30 minutes, turning a few times, or until thoroughly browned on both sides.

Add the beets, parsnips, onion, celery, garlic, bay leaf, rosemary, port, and chocolate and stir well. Add just enough broth to cover all the ingredients. Season with salt and pepper to taste.

≫ ≫ ≫ ≫

Bring to a boil, then reduce the heat to low and simmer, uncovered, for about 2 hours, or until the roast is very tender when tested with a knife. During the cooking process, add more broth as needed to cover the roast halfway up the sides.

Using large slotted spoons, transfer the roast and vegetables to a large warmed platter.

If the sauce is thin, cook over medium heat to reduce it to a gravy. Spoon on top of the meat and vegetables on the platter.

Garnish with the parsley and serve with a large fork and spoon to tear the meat apart.

calves' liver with mushroom-onion ragout

Liver is delicious and a great source of iron. I love it smothered in lots of onions with bits of salty bacon and, as my father ate it, dipped in plenty of tomato catsup. When possible, buy liver from naturally raised calves, which has a better flavor.

variation: To turn this into a complete meal, just before returning the liver to the pot, add a few diced carrots and potatoes along with a little chicken broth or water. Simmer 15 minutes longer, or until the vegetables are tender.

8 thick slices bacon

1½ cups fine dried bread crumbs

4 tablespoons minced fresh flat-leaf parsley

2 teaspoons salt

½ teaspoon freshly ground pepper

2 pounds calves' liver, cut into ½-inch-thick diagonal slices

MUSHROOM-onion RaGOUT

2 onions, thinly sliced

8 ounces button mushrooms, thinly sliced

2 to 3 tablespoons red wine vinegar

⅓ cup tomato catsup

1 cup chicken broth or water

Salt and freshly ground pepper to taste

SERVES 4

In a large, heavy skillet, cook the bacon over medium heat until crisp. Using a slotted spoon, remove the bacon and transfer to paper towels. Chop the bacon into ½-inch pieces.

In a shallow bowl, combine the bread crumbs, 3 tablespoons of parsley, salt, and pepper. Rinse the liver in cold water and thoroughly coat it in the seasoned bread crumbs.

Pour off and reserve all but about 2 tablespoons of the bacon fat in the skillet. Heat the fat in the skillet over medium heat. Add the liver slices in batches so that you can turn them with ease. Cook each batch until browned, 3 to 4 minutes on each side, or until an instant-read thermometer inserted in the center of a slice registers 140°F.

During cooking, add a little more bacon fat when needed, but reserve a few tablespoons for the ragout. Using a metal spatula, transfer the liver to a large platter and set aside.

To make the ragout, heat the reserved bacon fat over medium-low heat. Add the onions and mushrooms and cook, stirring occasionally, for 5 minutes.

Add the vinegar, catsup, and broth. Increase the heat to medium, cover, and cook for 20 to 30 minutes, or until the ragout thickens slightly. Taste and adjust the seasoning.

Just before serving, return the liver to the skillet, placing it on top of the ragout. Cover and cook over medium heat for 3 to 5 minutes, or until the liver is warmed through.

To serve, transfer the liver slices to a platter or divide among warmed plates. Spoon the ragout around and on top of the liver. Garnish with the bacon, then sprinkle with the remaining parsley.

Beef Stew with Buttermilk Dumplings

This rich-tasting dish is my take on the traditional French boeuf bourguignon. To turn it into a one-pot meal, fluffy, easy-to-make buttermilk dumplings are poached in the wine-tinged braising liquid toward the end of the cooking process. This one only gets better the next day, which is a good thing, since you'll probably have enough for leftovers. You can also double the recipe and freeze half for later use.

variation: Delete the dumplings. Serve the stew in hollowed-out crusty rolls or over mashed potatoes or buttered noodles.

1 cup all-purpose flour

1 teaspoon salt, plus more to taste

2 pounds well-marbled beef stew meat (chuck, bottom round, or short rib), cut into 1-inch chunks

2 tablespoons olive oil

1 onion, coarsely chopped

1 cup coarsely chopped fennel

¾ cup finely diced carrot

2 cups dry red wine, such as Zinfandel, Sangiovese, Cabernet, or Merlot

2 cups beef broth

1 large rutabaga, peeled and cut into ½-inch pieces (2 cups)

3 cloves garlic, minced

2 tablespoons coarsely chopped fresh marjoram

Freshly ground pepper to taste

BUTTERMILK DUMPLINGS

1½ cups all-purpose flour

2 teaspoons baking powder

½ teaspoon salt

3 tablespoons unsalted butter, cut into small pieces

1 cup buttermilk

2 tablespoons minced fresh chives for garnish

SERVES 4 TO 6

In a large bowl, combine the flour and the 1 teaspoon of salt. Add the beef chunks in batches and toss to coat evenly, shaking off the excess flour. Set aside.

In a large, heavy pot, heat the olive oil over medium heat and cook the meat, in batches if necessary, turning occasionally, until browned on all sides, about 10 minutes.

Add the onion, fennel, carrot, wine, and beef broth. Bring to a boil, then reduce the heat to low and simmer, uncovered, for 1 to 1½ hours, or until the meat is very tender and the stewing liquid is thick and flavorful.

Add the rutabaga, garlic, marjoram, and salt and pepper to taste. Simmer, uncovered, for another 20 minutes, or until the rutabaga is tender.

Just before serving, make the dumplings: In a medium bowl, combine the flour, baking powder, and salt. Cut the butter into pea-sized pieces and, using your hands or a pastry cutter, blend the butter into the flour mixture until it resembles coarse meal. Stir in the buttermilk to form a soft batter.

Increase the heat to medium-low. Using a large tablespoon, gently push all of the stew ingredients toward the bottom of the pot to make room on the top. Grease a tablespoon with some oil, then drop rounded tablespoonfuls of dough into the simmering stew. Cover and cook for about 15 minutes, or until the dumplings rise slightly. Uncover and use a slotted spoon to transfer the dumplings to a platter.

To serve, divide the stew and dumplings among 4 to 6 warmed bowls; garnish with the chives. Or, to serve family style, ladle the stew into a deep serving dish, place the dumplings on top, and sprinkle with the chives.

MEAT LOaF WITH POTaTOES anD STEaMED GREEN BEans

Here's a creative way to make a meat loaf without having to turn on your oven. The green beans are steamed on top of the meat loaf during the last few minutes of cooking. When the meat loaf is inverted onto the platter, the potatoes form a nicely browned crust.

VARIATIONS: Instead of green beans, use another seasonal vegetable, such as broccoli, cauliflower, zucchini, or corn, cooking it to the desired doneness.

2 pounds ground beef, or a combination of half beef and half pork or ground turkey
1 onion, shredded
1 large carrot, peeled and shredded
4 ounces button mushrooms, coarsely chopped

1 cup dried bread crumbs
1 tablespoon dried Italian herbs
2 large eggs, lightly beaten
1 teaspoon salt, plus more to taste
½ teaspoon freshly ground pepper, plus more to taste

1 tablespoon Worcestershire sauce
1 large russet potato, peeled and cut into very thin slices, preferably on a mandoline
3 tablespoons olive oil
8 ounces green beans, trimmed

SERVES 6

In a large bowl, combine the ground meat, onion, carrot, mushrooms, bread crumbs, herbs, eggs, 1 teaspoon salt, ½ teaspoon pepper, and the Worcestershire sauce. Using your hands, mix everything together thoroughly.

In a medium bowl, toss the potato slices with 1 tablespoon of the olive oil until well coated. Season them with salt and pepper to taste.

Cut 2 pieces of parchment paper or aluminum foil to fit the bottom of a nonstick or generously oiled 8-quart pot. Use the remaining olive oil to thoroughly oil the pot.

Arrange a single layer of overlapping potato slices on the top of the paper or foil. Spoon the meat loaf mixture on top of the potatoes and, using your hands, push it down firmly to form a gently rounded mound. Cover and cook over low heat for about 45 minutes, or until an instant-read thermometer inserted in the middle reads 160°F.

Just before you remove the meat loaf, turn off the heat, uncover, and place the green beans on top of the meat loaf. Cover again and steam for about 2 minutes, or until the beans are bright green and crisp-tender. Using tongs, transfer the beans to a small serving bowl and season them with salt and pepper to taste.

Invert the pot over a warmed large, deep platter, shaking the pot slightly to remove the meat loaf. Cut the meat loaf into wedges and serve with the beans.

MY MOM'S BEEF BRISKET WITH PRUNES AND APRICOTS

I was brought up Jewish, and every Passover, our holiday table was graced with my mom's savory brisket of beef. She seasoned it with a couple of packages of dried onion soup and lots of catsup. I still use the catsup, but I substitute real onions for the onion soup mix and add espresso, which imparts a deep richness. Braising a whole brisket takes several hours, but the reward is a hearty meal with lots of leftovers.

SERVING SUGGESTION: Serve over buttered noodles that have been boiled separately or cooked in the cooking liquid in the same pot.

Salt to taste, plus 1 tablespoon
Freshly ground pepper to taste, plus 1 teaspoon
One 3- to 5-pound beef brisket
3 large onions, thinly sliced
4 cloves garlic, minced
2 bay leaves

2 cups dry red wine
2 cups catsup
½ cup brewed espresso or strong dark coffee
8 to 16 cups beef broth
4 ounces dried apricots
4 ounces pitted prunes

SERVES 6 TO 8

Generously season the meat with salt and pepper to taste. In a large, heavy pot, combine the brisket, onions, garlic, bay leaves, red wine, catsup, espresso, 1 tablespoon salt, and 1 teaspoon pepper and stir well. Add 6 cups of the beef broth. Cover and simmer over medium-low heat for 2 hours, adding more broth as needed to keep the brisket half submerged.

Uncover and simmer for 1 hour, or until tender when tested with a knife. Using a large spoon, skim off and discard as much fat as possible.

≫ ≫ ≫ ≫

Add the apricots and prunes and simmer, uncovered, 1 hour longer. At this point, the brisket should be very tender when tested or sliced with a knife.

Using tongs, transfer the brisket to a cutting board. With a slotted spoon, transfer the fruit to a small bowl.

If the sauce is thin, cook it over high heat to reduce to the desired consistency. Remove the bay leaves and season to taste with salt and pepper.

Slice the meat against the grain into ½-inch-thick slices. Return to the pot with the fruit to reheat if necessary.

Serve on a large platter or warmed plates. Ladle the sauce and fruit over the meat or serve on the side.

SHORT RIBS WITH STEAMED SEASONAL VEGETABLES

This dish is a perfect example of the ideal one-pot meal. The short ribs need to be slowly cooked for several hours, but just before serving a few handfuls of seasonal vegetables are steamed in the same pot, either in a steamer basket or right on top of the meat. The cooking time will depend on the type of vegetable you choose. To add even more flavor, toss the vegetables with a little salt, pepper, and fresh herbs or lemon zest before steaming.

SERVING SUGGESTIONS: This dish would be great with polenta, mashed potatoes, or mashed cauliflower. Or, slice the meat and serve warm or chilled in sandwiches with horseradish and mayonnaise.

4 pounds bone-in beef short ribs

3 tablespoons garam masala

Salt and freshly ground pepper to taste

2 tablespoons olive oil

6 shallots, thinly sliced

2 carrots, peeled and cut into
    ½-inch-thick slices

½ cup chopped Italian parsley

½ cup chopped fresh oregano

8 whole peppercorns, crushed

3 cloves garlic, chopped

One 8-ounce can tomato paste

2 cups ruby port

About 4 cups chicken broth

About 4 cups mixed chopped or sliced
    seasonal vegetables

SERVES 4 TO 6

In a medium bowl, toss the ribs in the garam masala and season generously with salt and pepper.

In a large, heavy pot, heat the olive oil over medium-high heat. Add the ribs in batches and brown thoroughly on all sides for about 15 minutes. Return all the ribs to the pot and add the shallots, carrots, parsley, oregano, peppercorns, and garlic. Cook for 10 minutes, or until the vegetables are lightly browned.

≫ ≫ ≫ ≫

In a small bowl, combine the tomato paste and port and add it to the pot. Add 3 cups of the chicken broth and season with salt and pepper to taste. Bring the liquid to a boil, then reduce the heat to medium-low and simmer, covered, turning the ribs occasionally with tongs, until they are very tender and nearly falling off the bones, 2 to 3 hours. Add extra liquid as needed to keep the ribs halfway submerged.

Transfer the ribs and carrots to a platter. Strain the pan juices through a fine-meshed sieve into a medium bowl. Return the juice to the pot and cook over medium-high heat for 10 to 15 minutes, or until thickened to the consistency of a light gravy. Taste and adjust the seasoning.

Five or ten minutes before serving, put the ribs back into the juices and heat through over medium-low heat. At this time add the vegetables to a steamer basket inserted into the pot or place them directly on top of the ribs. Reduce the heat to low, cover, and cook dense vegetables like potatoes for 15 to 20 minutes, or until tender, or vegetables like zucchini and green beans for 4 or 5 minutes, or until crisp-tender.

To serve, arrange the short ribs on a large platter or warmed individual plates. Surround with the vegetables and spoon the extra sauce over the ribs.

corned Beef and cabbage

You don't have to wait for St. Patrick's Day to have a pot of corned beef and cabbage simmering on your stove. In fact, my dad, who didn't have a drop of Irish blood in him, absolutely adored corned beef. The secret ingredient here is a malty beer whose alcohol content cooks off long before it arrives at the table.

Plan on making this dish when you are staying home all day. Although it takes very little time to prepare, the beef must be cooked for hours to tenderize it.

serving suggestion: Corned beef is a large cut of beef, so you will end up with leftovers, which will be welcome around your house for days. Slice the corned beef and serve it warm or cold for sandwiches or chopped with potatoes and onions as a great breakfast hash.

One 3- to 5-pound corned beef
8 whole peppercorns
3 bay leaves
2 onions, thinly sliced
2 bottles dark ale
3 carrots, peeled and cut into ½-inch-thick slices

3 turnips, peeled and cut into ½-inch-thick wedges
6 unpeeled white- or golden-fleshed boiling potatoes, cut into ½-inch chunks
1 cabbage, cored and cut into 6 wedges
Salt and freshly ground pepper to taste
Pinch of sugar

1 small bunch Swiss chard, thinly sliced
Honey mustard, horseradish mixed with a little sour cream, and/or chopped green onions for serving (optional)

SERVES 6 TO 8

Put the corned beef in a very large, heavy pot and add water to cover it completely. Bring the water to a boil, then reduce the heat to medium-low and simmer for 1 hour.

Using tongs, transfer the corned beef to a large platter. Discard the water, return the corned beef to the pot, and again add water to cover completely. Add the peppercorns, bay leaves, onions, and ale. Bring to a boil, then reduce the heat to low, cover, and simmer for about 4 hours, or until fork-tender. Using a small ladle, skim off any excess fat on the surface of the sauce.

Add the carrots and turnips and simmer, uncovered, for 1 more hour. Add the potatoes and cabbage and simmer 30 minutes longer. Season with salt, pepper, and sugar.

Just before serving, turn off the heat, add the Swiss chard, cover, and cook until wilted, about 5 minutes.

Using tongs, transfer the chard to a small bowl. Transfer the corned beef to a cutting board and let rest for 5 minutes. Cut the meat against the grain into ¼-inch-thick slices and arrange them on a large platter or in warmed shallow bowls. Ladle the juices and vegetables on top.

If you like, serve with small bowls filled with honey mustard, horseradish mixed with sour cream, and chopped green onions.

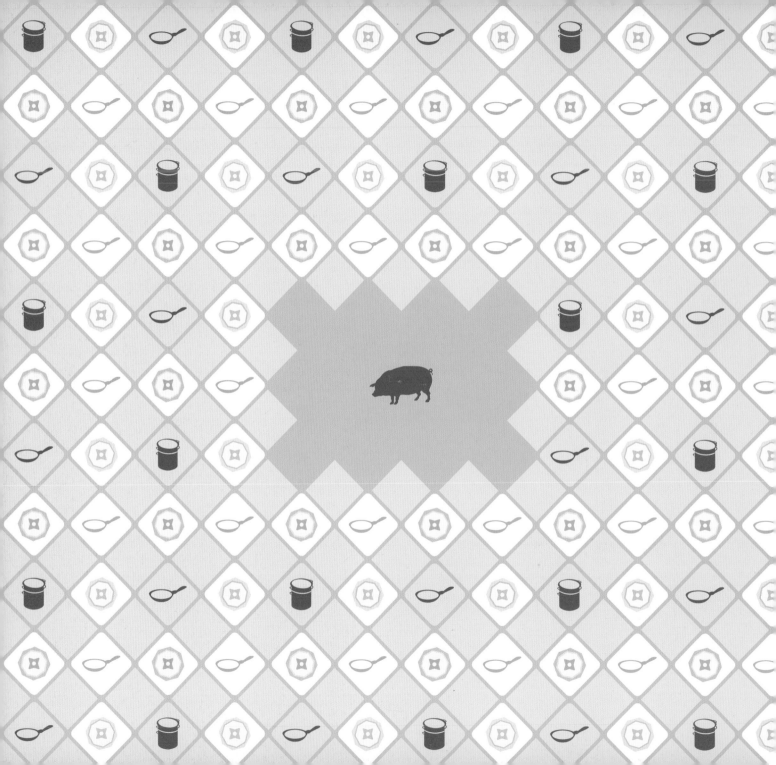

PORK

MOnTAnA-STYLe POrK anD WHITe Bean STEW

This gussied-up version of pork and beans was inspired by Jeff Miller, the executive chef at Papoose Creek Eco Lodge in Cameron, Montana. I spent a week at the lodge as a guest chef and learning how to fly-fish. Although the kitchen at the lodge prepares what is considered fairly upscale fare for Big Sky country, there is an element of hearty, straightforward good ol' Montana in every dish, including this one. This twist on a classic recipe will yield you plenty of leftovers, which will taste even better the next day.

Serving Suggestion: Serve with warm corn bread or spooned over gourmet hot dogs for the ultimate chili dog.

2 cups dried cannellini beans, soaked overnight and drained, or 6 cups canned cannellini beans, drained

¼ cup olive oil

2 pounds pork butt (pork shoulder), trimmed and cut into 1-inch pieces

Salt and freshly ground pepper to taste

4 ounces pancetta, cut into 2-inch strips

1 leek, white and light green parts only, rinsed and thinly sliced

1 stalk celery, cut into ¼-inch dice

1 carrot, peeled and cut into ¼-inch dice

1 small fennel bulb, cored and cut into ¼-inch dice

1 bay leaf

1 teaspoon fennel seeds

1 poblano chili, seeded and coarsely chopped

1 jalapeño chili, seeded and minced

4 cloves garlic, minced

2 tablespoons tomato paste

1 cup dry white wine

4 to 6 cups chicken broth

1 tablespoon minced fresh rosemary

1 tablespoon grated lemon zest

SERVES 6, WITH LEFTOVERS

If using dried beans, place them in a large saucepan, add water to cover by 2 inches, and simmer, uncovered, for 30 minutes. Drain and set aside.

In a large, heavy pot, heat the olive oil over medium heat. Lightly season the pork with salt and pepper and cook in batches, turning occasionally, for about 10 minutes, or until browned on all sides. Using a slotted spoon, transfer the pork to a medium bowl and set aside.

» » » »

To the same pot, add the pancetta, leek, celery, carrot, fennel, bay leaf, fennel seeds, and chilies. Reduce the heat to medium-low and cook for about 5 minutes, or until softened. Stir in the garlic and tomato paste and cook 1 minute longer.

Add the beans and return the pork to the pot. Add the wine, 4 cups of broth, the rosemary, and lemon zest and season with salt and pepper to taste. Bring the stew to a boil, then reduce the heat to medium, cover, and simmer for about 1½ hours, stirring occasionally and adding more broth if necessary. The sauce should be thick and the meat should be fork-tender.

To serve, ladle into warmed bowls.

FARMER'S PORK CHOWDER

Chowder is a perfect one-pot meal because it is such a substantial dish. I found the inspiration for this recipe in a cookbook written in 1904 called *The Modern Cook Book and Household Recipes.* It's a fine example of how versatile chowder can be.

SERVING SUGGESTION: In keeping with the American theme, serve this dish with wedges of iceburg lettuce topped with a blue cheese or Thousand Island dressing.

8 slices bacon, cut into 1-inch strips

1½ pounds boneless pork butt (pork shoulder), cut into 1-inch cubes, or 1½ pounds pork stew meat

1 onion, coarsely chopped

1½ pounds unpeeled boiling potatoes, thickly sliced

2 cups water

2 cups milk

¼ cup all-purpose flour

1 cup fresh or frozen corn kernels

½ red bell pepper, seeded and finely diced

2 tablespoons minced fresh flat-leaf parsley

Salt and freshly ground pepper to taste

1 teaspoon sweet paprika for garnish

SERVES 4 TO 6

In a large, heavy pot, fry the bacon over medium heat for about 5 minutes, or until brown and slightly crisp. Add the pork, onion, and potatoes and cook for about 5 minutes to lightly brown the potatoes.

Add the water, cover, and reduce to medium-low heat. Simmer for about 1 hour, or until fork-tender.

In a medium bowl, whisk ½ cup of the milk with the flour until blended. Add to the pot along with the remaining 1½ cups milk.

Simmer, uncovered, for about 5 minutes, or until thickened slightly. Add the corn and bell pepper and simmer for another 5 minutes. Add the parsley, salt, and pepper.

To serve, ladle the chowder into a large, deep serving bowl or into warmed shallow bowls and garnish with a sprinkle of paprika.

BRaISeD COUNTRY PORK RIBS WITH WHeaT BeRRIeS

Braising pork ribs in an oniony, sage-tinged liquid results in rich, tender, falling-off-the-bone meat. I love to pair them with wheat berries, which are not only good for you but, when prepared in the right way, are also delicious and deeply satisfying. Since you cook them directly in the pot along with the ribs, they will absorb the meaty flavors of the juices.

VARIATION: Although this dish already contains vegetables, just before serving you could add a few handfuls of chopped chard or bok choy to the pot and cook for 5 minutes.

2 tablespoons olive oil
2 pounds country pork ribs
Salt and freshly ground pepper to taste
1 onion, thinly sliced

1 fennel bulb, cored and thinly sliced
2 parsnips, peeled and cut into ½-inch-thick rounds
3 cloves garlic, minced

3 cups chicken broth
1 cup wheat berries
3 tablespoons minced fresh flat-leaf parsley
3 tablespoons minced fresh sage

SERVES 4

In a large, heavy pot, heat the olive oil over medium heat. Lightly season the pork with salt and pepper and cook, turning as needed, for about 10 minutes, or until nicely browned. Using tongs, transfer the pork to a large platter.

Do not wipe out the pot, but add the onion, fennel, parsnips, and garlic and sauté over medium-low heat for about 5 minutes to slightly soften the vegetables.

Return the pork ribs to the pot along with the chicken broth and wheat berries. Season with salt and pepper to taste. Cover and cook for 1½ to 2 hours, or until the pork is fork-tender. During cooking, turn the ribs and stir the sauce occasionally.

To serve, arrange the pork ribs on a large platter or in warmed individual shallow bowls. Add the parsley and sage to the pot and stir. Spoon the vegetables, wheat berries, and juices on top of the ribs.

BRAISED CHIPOTLE-ORANGE PORK WITH YAMS

The tangy and spicy glaze of this slow-cooked roast pairs wonderfully with the pork's natural sweetness. Although a large roast like this is traditionally cooked in the oven, here it's braised on the stove top, allowing the intoxicating aromas to fill the kitchen.

SERVING SUGGESTION: This roast is delectable on its own, but I like to serve it with little bowls of cooling garnishes, such as chopped cilantro, avocado, red onion, red bell pepper, and crumbled feta cheese.

½ cup all-purpose flour
1½ tablespoons ground cumin
1 tablespoon ground coriander
1½ teaspoons salt
½ teaspoon freshly ground pepper
One 3- to 5-pound pork butt (pork shoulder)
2 tablespoons olive oil

3 leeks, white parts only, rinsed and thickly sliced
2 carrots, peeled and thinly sliced
2 chipotle chilies en adobo, minced
1 tablespoon adobo sauce from chipotles
2 tablespoons packed brown sugar
1 tablespoon whole-grain mustard

1 tablespoon Worcestershire sauce
3 whole cloves
1 pound yams, peeled and cut into 2-inch cubes
2 tablespoons grated orange zest
⅔ cup orange juice
1 cup chicken broth

SERVES 6, WITH LEFTOVERS

In a large bowl, combine the flour, cumin, coriander, salt, and pepper. Add the pork and toss well to thoroughly coat with the seasoned flour.

In a large, heavy pot, heat the olive oil over medium heat, add the pork, and cook, turning every 5 minutes, until browned on all sides, about 20 minutes. Using tongs, transfer the pork to a platter.

Add all the remaining ingredients to the pot and stir well. Reduce the heat to medium-low and simmer, uncovered, for about 10 minutes. Return the pork roast to the pot.

Cover and cook for about 1 hour, or until an instant-read thermometer inserted in the center of the meat registers 160°F. Transfer the pork to a cutting board and cut into ½-inch-thick slices.

To serve, taste and adjust the seasoning. Using a large spoon, transfer the vegetables to a large platter or warmed plates. Arrange the pork slices on top and spoon more juices over the pork.

PORK OSSO BUCO WITH SWISS CHARD

Osso buco is traditionally made with veal and braised in the oven. In this version, I substitute pork shanks, cut in the same manner so that the exposed sweet bone marrow can melt and mingle with the rest of the ingredients. Ask your butcher to cut the shanks for osso buco (see below).

VARIATION AND SERVING SUGGESTION: Although the pork is cooked with carrots, fennel, and onion, I like to add a bunch of coarsely sliced Swiss chard, which can be cooked in a little olive oil in the same pot for 3 to 5 minutes after the pork and carrots are removed. As is, this is a perfect low-carbohydrate meal, but you could also serve it over a mound of creamy polenta or mashed potatoes.

2 to 3 tablespoons garam masala

1 teaspoon salt

¼ teaspoon freshly ground pepper

3 pounds pork shanks, cut crosswise on the diagonal into 2- to 3-inch pieces

3 tablespoons olive oil

1 onion, coarsely chopped

1 fennel bulb, trimmed, cored, and coarsely chopped

3 cloves garlic, minced

2 carrots, peeled and cut into eighths lengthwise

2 cups ruby port

1 large bay leaf

2 to 3 cups chicken broth

2 tablespoons unsalted butter

SERVES 4

In a large bowl, combine the garam masala, salt, and pepper. Add the pork and toss to season well.

In a large, heavy pot, heat 2 tablespoons of the olive oil over medium heat. Add the pork and cook, turning frequently, until the meat is brown on all sides, about 20 minutes.

» » » »

Add the onion, fennel, garlic, carrots, port, bay leaf, and 2 cups chicken broth. Bring to a boil, then reduce the heat to low, cover, and simmer for about 1½ hours, or until the pork is fork-tender. While the pork is simmering, add more chicken broth if necessary to keep the pork about halfway submerged in liquid.

Using tongs, transfer the pork and carrots to a large platter. Cover with aluminum foil to keep warm.

Strain the juices through a fine-meshed sieve and return to the pot. Whisk the butter into the juices and simmer for about another 2 minutes, or until the sauce thickens slightly. Taste and adjust the seasoning.

To serve, place the pork and carrots on a platter or warmed plates and pour the sauce over.

STUFFED PORK CHOPS WITH CALVADOS AND JUNIPER BERRY SAUCE

This dish is a pork-lover's dream. The chops are stuffed with pork sausage and apples, then wrapped in bacon. Calvados, an apple brandy, blended with a touch of cream and a hint of juniper berries, makes a delicious accompanying sauce. If you want a lighter version, substitute more chicken broth for the cream.

SERVING SUGGESTION: This dish would be great served with boiled potatoes. Simply cook the potatoes in the pot before you cook the pork chops, then pour the piping hot Calvados sauce on top of them to reheat slightly at serving time.

4 double-cut boneless pork chops
(8 to 10 ounces each)

STUFFING
2 tart cooking apples, such as Pippin, Granny Smith, or Fuji, peeled and cored
1 sweet Italian sausage

2 tablespoons shredded red onion
1 clove garlic, minced

Salt and freshly ground pepper to taste
8 strips bacon
2 tablespoons olive oil
1 tablespoon minced fresh thyme

3 juniper berries, crushed
2 cups chicken broth
½ cup Calvados or other apple brandy
½ cup heavy cream
1 green onion, including green parts, coarsely chopped

SERVES 4

Using a small, sharp knife, slice the pork chops horizontally three-fourths of the way through the center, leaving one side uncut, to make a pocket for the stuffing.

To make the stuffing: Cut 1½ of the apples into ¼-inch-thick slices and set aside in a small bowl. Shred the remaining ½ apple and set aside in a medium bowl. Remove the sausage from the casing and chop coarsely. Add the sausage, onion, and garlic to the shredded apple. Mix well. Fill the cavity of each chop with one-fourth of the stuffing. Using your hands, gently press each pork chop to compress the filling inside.

Season each chop lightly with salt and pepper. Wrap the outside of each pork chop with 2 strips of bacon, securing them with toothpicks.

In a large, heavy skillet, heat the olive oil over medium-high heat, add the pork chops, and cook for 5 minutes on each side, or until the bacon is browned.

Add the thyme, juniper berries, and chicken broth to the skillet. Bring to a simmer, cover, and reduce the heat to very low and cook the chops, uncovered, turning them occasionally, until an instant-read thermometer inserted in the center of the chops reads 185°F, about 1 hour.

Transfer the pork chops to a platter and cover with aluminum foil to keep them warm.

Add the Calvados, heavy cream, and three-fourths of the sliced apples to the skillet. Increase the heat to medium-high and simmer for about 15 minutes, or until the liquid thickens.

To serve, using tongs, place the pork chops on a large platter or warmed plates. Pour the brandy sauce over the chops and garnish with the chopped green onion and remaining apple slices.

PORK CHOPS WITH SWEET AND SPICY RED CABBAGE AND STEAMED DILL DUMPLINGS

Pork chops and braised red cabbage go hand in hand, and in this recipe, they go together literally, as they are cooked together in the same pot. To make this a complete meal, the dumplings are cooked right on top of the pork chops.

Dumplings are easier to make than you may think and are a wonderful, comforting accompaniment. I prefer to make them oversized. The next day, split them in half and warm in a little butter before spooning the reheated pork and cabbage on top.

VARIATION: Instead of dumplings, serve this dish with buttered noodles or potato salad.

2 tablespoons olive oil

Salt and freshly ground pepper to taste

4 double-cut pork chops (8 to 10 ounces each)

1 red onion, very thinly sliced

½ red cabbage, cored and shredded

½ cup seasoned rice wine vinegar

¼ cup packed brown sugar

½ teaspoon red pepper flakes, or
   1½ teaspoons minced fresh chili

DUMPLINGS

4 tablespoons unsalted butter, softened

1 egg, beaten

1 cup all-purpose flour

⅛ teaspoon salt

2 tablespoons minced fresh dill

6 to 8 tablespoons milk

1 cup chicken broth

1 tablespoon minced fresh dill for garnish

½ cup sour cream

SERVES 4

In a large, heavy pot, heat the olive oil over medium heat. Lightly salt and pepper the pork chops, then cook, turning occasionally, until browned, about 10 minutes. Transfer the pork chops to a large platter and set aside.

Add the onion and cabbage to the pot, reduce the heat to medium-low, and cook, stirring occasionally, for about 10 minutes, or until the vegetables are softened. Add the vinegar, sugar, and red pepper flakes and stir well.

While the cabbage is simmering, make the dumpling batter: In a medium bowl, combine the butter and egg. Add the flour, salt, dill, and enough milk to form a stiff batter. Divide the dough into 8 to 10 pieces. Using floured hands, flatten each piece slightly, forming them into ¼-inch-thick silver dollar–sized disks.

Return the pork chops to the pot, pushing them down into the cabbage. Pour in the broth and bring to a boil. Arrange the dumplings on top, using a spoon to push them down slightly into the simmering liquid. Cover, reduce the heat to low, and simmer for about 15 minutes, or until the dumplings are cooked through and an instant-read thermometer reads 155ºF to 165ºF when inserted in the center of the pork.

To serve, transfer the dumplings to a large platter or 4 warmed plates. Spoon the cabbage and pork chops next to the dumplings and drizzle a generous amount of the juices over all. Garnish with the dill and dollops of the sour cream.

PORK TENDERLOIN WITH BALSAMIC PEACHES AND GOAT CHEESE

The wonders of one-pot cooking extend to fast-cooking recipes like this summery pork tenderloin. Take care not to overcook this tender cut of meat. It will be at its best cooked to medium-rare.

VARIATION AND SERVING SUGGESTION: For a wintertime variation, used drained canned peaches. This dish would be wonderful paired with the light bitterness of an arugula salad.

2 tablespoons olive oil
Two 1-pound pork tenderloins
Salt and freshly ground pepper to taste
1 red onion, thinly sliced
1 cup chicken broth

¼ cup packed brown sugar
2 tablespoons stone-ground mustard
3 tablespoons balsamic vinegar
1 cinnamon stick, broken into 3 or 4 pieces

2 firm, ripe peaches, peeled, pitted, and cut
    into ½-inch-thick slices
4 to 6 ounces soft goat cheese
1 tablespoon minced fresh flat-leaf parsley
    for garnish

SERVES 4 TO 6

In a large, heavy pot, heat the olive oil over medium heat. Season the pork with salt and pepper and cook, turning occasionally, until brown on all sides, about 10 minutes. Transfer to a platter and loosely cover with aluminum foil.

Reduce the heat to medium-low and cook the onions in the same pot for 5 minutes, or until softened. Add the broth, brown sugar, mustard, balsamic vinegar, and cinnamon pieces. Bring to a boil, then reduce the heat to medium-low and simmer for 5 minutes to marry the flavors. Add the peaches and simmer for another 5 minutes.

Return the tenderloins to the pot, cover, and cook for another 10 to 15 minutes, or until an instant-read thermometer inserted in the middle of the meat registers from 145°F to 150°F.

Using tongs, transfer the tenderloins to a cutting board and let rest for 5 minutes. Cut crosswise into ½-inch-thick slices.

To serve, spoon the peaches onto a large platter or warmed plates and crumble the goat cheese over them. Arrange the pork slices on top of the peaches down the center of the plate and garnish with the parsley.

MRS. Dent's Italian sausage and chicken stew

A childhood neighbor, Mrs. Dent, was one of the best rustic Italian cooks I have ever met. She made this stew and served it over polenta. The next day, she would strain off the excess juices, scramble the leftover stew with a few eggs, and tuck it into crusty rolls for lunch. This is a wonderful, healthful dish during summer, when tomatoes and basil are at their best.

serving suggestion: This stew would also be delicious ladled over rice or pasta (or, Mrs. Dent style, over polenta), which can be made ahead of time in the same pot.

2 tablespoons olive oil

1 pound sweet or hot Italian sausages, cut into 1-inch-thick slices

2 large boneless, skinless chicken breasts, or 4 boned thighs (1 to 1½ pounds)

1 red bell pepper, seeded and cut into ½-inch-thick slices

1 yellow onion, thinly sliced

4 to 6 cloves garlic, minced

2 very ripe tomatoes, seeded and coarsely chopped, or one 14-ounce can chopped tomatoes

2 tablespoons minced fresh oregano

½ cup dry red wine

1 cup thinly sliced fresh basil

Salt and freshly ground pepper to taste

½ cup (2 ounces) grated Asiago cheese for garnish

SERVES 4, WITH LEFTOVERS

In a large, heavy skillet, heat the olive oil over medium heat and cook the sausage and chicken, turning occasionally, until lightly browned on all sides, about 8 minutes. Add the red pepper, onion, garlic, tomatoes, oregano, red wine, and ½ cup of the basil. Reduce the heat to medium-low, cover, and simmer for 15 minutes, or until the chicken is opaque throughout. Stir in the remaining basil. Season with salt and pepper.

To serve, spoon onto a large platter or warmed plates and sprinkle with the grated cheese.

all-american alfredo

As a restaurant owner and chef, I am often asked what I most like to eat when I cook for myself at home. More often than I like to admit, it is some kind of humble egg dish, like this one, which is essentially a glorified version of ham and eggs served over noodles cooked ahead of time in the same pot. For a lower-fat version, substitute chicken broth for the cream.

variation: For an Alfredo with vegetables, add 1 cup of green peas or chopped broccoli when you put the pasta back into the pot. Just before serving, place slices of fresh tomato on top of the creamy pasta. Cover the pot with a lid for a few minutes to warm the tomatoes.

12 ounces dried broad egg noodles
1 tablespoon light olive oil
2 tablespoons unsalted butter
8 eggs, beaten
Salt and freshly ground pepper to taste

12 to 14 ounces ham steak, trimmed and cut into 1-inch-long matchsticks
5 green onions, including green parts, coarsely chopped
1 tablespoon minced fresh oregano

1 cup heavy cream
1 cup (4 ounces) shredded sharp Cheddar cheese

SERVES 4

In a large pot of salted boiling water, cook the noodles for 8 to 12 minutes, or until al dente. Drain and rinse the noodles under cold water. Toss with the olive oil and set aside.

In the same pot, melt the butter over medium heat. Add the eggs. Do not scramble, but using a spatula, turn occasionally to cook the eggs thoroughly. Coarsely chop them into bite-sized pieces. Season the eggs with salt and pepper. Using a slotted spoon, transfer the egg pieces to a small bowl.

In the same pot, combine the ham, three-fourths of the green onions, the oregano, and cream. Simmer over medium-low heat for 5 minutes.

Just before serving, reduce the heat to low and return the eggs and pasta to the pot. Add three-fourths of the Cheddar cheese. Using a large wooden spoon or tongs, toss the ingredients and continue to cook for a few minutes more to melt the cheese. Season with salt and pepper to taste.

To serve, scoop the mixture onto a large platter or warmed plates. Sprinkle with the remaining Cheddar cheese and green onions.

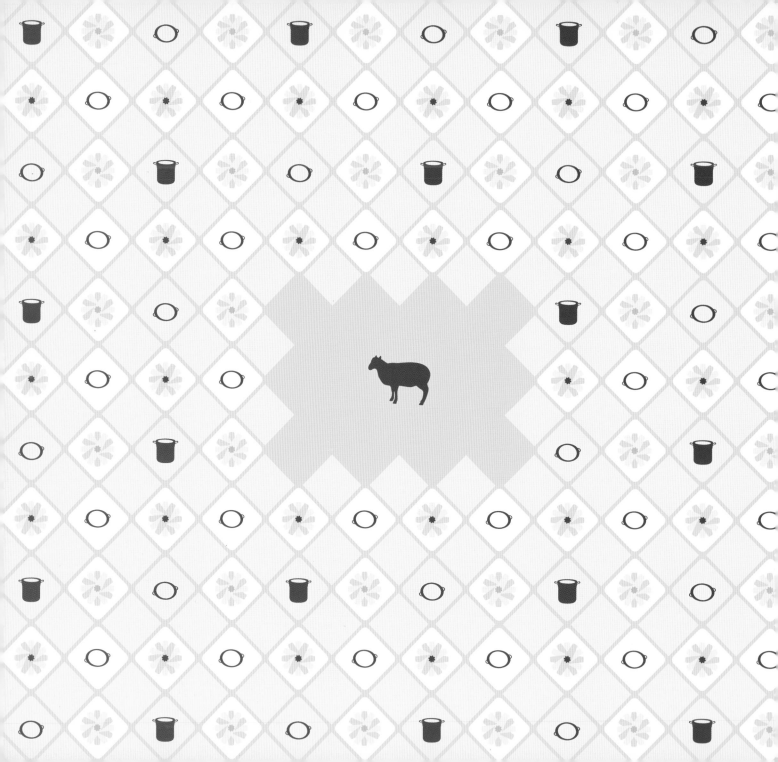

LAMB

Zinfandel-Braised Lamb Shanks with Red Lentils and Rice

This is an adaptation from a recipe in *The Versatile Grain and the Elegant Bean*, by Sheryl and Mel London (1992, Simon and Schuster). The combination of lentils and rice cooked in the savory juices of the braised lamb is exquisite.

The lamb shanks require a good three hours to absorb the flavors of the Zinfandel, juniper berries, and spices and become seductively tender. When I cook a recipe that takes hours, like this one, I often double it.

This is an ideal do-ahead dish for entertaining, since the flavors only get better over time and the shanks reheat well. You could call this the ultimate one-pot, one-bottle meal, since I recommend you serve it with the same Zinfandel used in the cooking process.

variation: This dish would be wonderful with steamed kale or spinach, which could be added to the pot 5–10 minutes before serving.

4 small or 2 large lamb shanks (3 to 4 pounds total)
Salt and freshly ground pepper to taste
All-purpose flour for dusting
2 tablespoons olive oil
1 onion, coarsely chopped
6 juniper berries, crushed

6 cloves garlic, minced
1 tablespoon Dijon mustard
2 tablespoons packed brown sugar
3 tablespoons minced fresh oregano
1 bay leaf
3 cups Zinfandel wine
About 4 cups chicken broth

½ teaspoon cayenne pepper
1 teaspoon sweet paprika
½ cup red lentils
¼ cup long-grain white rice
Chopped fresh flat-leaf parsley for garnish

SERVES 4

In a large bowl, season the lamb shanks with salt and pepper and thoroughly dust with flour, shaking off the excess.

In a large, heavy pot, heat the olive oil over medium-high heat and brown the shanks for 20 minutes, turning occasionally. Transfer to a platter and set aside.

Add the onions, juniper berries, garlic, mustard, brown sugar, oregano, bay leaf, Zinfandel, and 2 cups of the chicken broth and bring to a boil. Reduce the heat to low, cover, and simmer for about 1½ hours, turning the shanks every 30 minutes with tongs. During this time, add more broth as necessary to keep the shanks half submerged. Uncover and continue to cook until the meat is very tender and pulls away from the bone easily, about 1 hour longer. Transfer the shanks to a platter and cover loosely with aluminum foil.

Using a large spoon, skim off any excess fat from the braising liquid. Measure the liquid and add more broth if necessary to make 3 cups. Return to pot. Add the cayenne, paprika, lentils, and rice. Bring to a boil, cover, reduce the heat to low, and simmer for 30 minutes, or until the lentils are tender but firm.

There should also be liquid in the pot. If needed, add a little broth. Add salt and pepper to taste.

Just before serving, return the shanks to the pot, cover, and rewarm over low heat for about 10 minutes.

To serve, ladle the rice and lentils into a large serving bowl or warmed shallow bowls and arrange the shanks on top. Garnish with the parsley and serve with soup spoons.

CURRIED LEG OF LAMB WITH APPLES AND RAITA

This is a wonderful way to cook a leg of lamb on the stove top, where you can keep an eye on it, making sure it is cooked exactly to your desired doneness. The long cooking process allows the lamb to absorb all the wonderful aromatic East Indian spices in the curry sauce. Make this for your next dinner party—it can be prepared ahead of time, and it looks irresistible and impressive served on a large platter, family style.

This recipe requires a pot large enough to hold the leg of lamb.

One 7-pound boneless leg of lamb, rolled
   and tied with kitchen twine
Salt and freshly ground pepper to taste
10 cloves garlic, cut into thin slivers
¼ cup olive oil
2 onions, coarsely chopped
2 tablespoons fennel seeds
2 tablespoons cumin seeds
2 tablespoons coriander seeds
½ tablespoon fenugreek seeds
½ tablespoon black peppercorns
2 whole cloves

½ cinnamon stick, broken in half
3 cardamom pods
1 small chili, seeded and minced (optional)
4 cups chicken broth, plus more as needed

RAITA

1 cup peeled and shredded cucumber
½ cup shredded red onion
1½ cups plain yogurt
1½ tablespoons minced fresh mint
Salt to taste

¼ cup minced fresh mint, plus sprigs
   for garnish
¼ cup minced fresh cilantro
1 pound unpeeled sweet potatoes or yams,
   cut into 1-inch cubes
1 apple, peeled, cored, and coarsely chopped
1 bunch chard, cleaned and coarsely chopped

SERVES 6 TO 8

Season the lamb generously with salt and pepper. Using a sharp knife, make small slits all over the lamb. Slip half of the garlic slivers into the slits.

In a large, heavy pot, heat the olive oil over medium-high heat and brown the lamb on all sides, turning occasionally, for about 20 minutes. Using tongs and a long fork, transfer the lamb to a platter.

Reduce the heat to medium. Add the remaining garlic, the onions, fennel, cumin, coriander, fenugreek, peppercorns, cloves, cinnamon stick, cardamom, and chili. Cook for about 5 minutes, or until the onion is softened.

Return the leg of lamb to the pot, add 3 cups of the chicken broth, and reduce the heat to low. Cover and simmer for about 2 hours, or until an instant-read thermometer inserted in the center of the meat registers 145°F to 150°F for medium-rare. Stir the sauce and turn the leg every 30 minutes while cooking, and add chicken broth as needed to keep about 2 cups in the pot.

Meanwhile, make the raita: In a small bowl, combine the cucumber, onion, yogurt, mint, and salt and stir to blend. Cover and refrigerate for up to 2 days before use.

Transfer the lamb to a large platter and cover loosely with aluminum foil.

Strain the braising liquid through a medium-meshed sieve, pressing on the solids with the back of a large spoon to push as much of the solids through as possible. Return to the pot. Add the minced mint, cilantro, sweet potatoes, apple, chard, and the remaining 1 cup chicken broth. Simmer, covered, for 20 to 30 minutes, or until the potatoes are soft.

To serve, transfer the lamb to a cutting board and slice crosswise into ¼-inch-thick slices. Arrange the lamb slices on a large platter or warmed plates. Spoon the sauce over the lamb. Garnish with mint sprigs and serve with the raita alongside.

TUNISIAN LAMB STEW WITH SPINACH AND BULGUR

This rich, spicy lamb stew, redolent with Tunisian spices, is an exotic and welcome addition to the table, be it for a family dinner or a fancy dinner party. I like to serve it with bulgur (also known as cracked wheat), which is another staple of Mediterranean and Middle Eastern cuisine, to soak up the delicious sauce. Look for bulgur and spices in specialty stores or Middle Eastern markets.

variation: If you want the bulgar to be fluffy and separate from the stew, cook it in the pot first, according to the directions on the package, transfer it to a bowl, and then proceed with the recipe.

2 pounds lamb stew meat, cut into
   1-inch chunks
Salt and freshly ground pepper to taste
1 cup all-purpose flour
2 tablespoons olive oil
1 yellow onion, finely chopped

3 cloves garlic, minced
3 tablespoons grated fresh ginger
2 teaspoons ground cumin
1 teaspoon ground coriander
1 teaspoon caraway seeds
¾ teaspoon red pepper flakes

3 tablespoons tomato paste
4 cups chicken broth
1 bunch spinach, washed and steamed
1 cup bulgur (cracked wheat)
Warm whole-wheat pita breads for serving

SERVES 4 TO 6

In a large bowl, season the lamb chunks with salt and pepper, then dust with the flour, shaking off the excess.

In a large, heavy pot, heat the olive oil over medium-high heat, then add the lamb and cook, turning occasionally, until the meat is brown on all sides, about 15 minutes. Transfer the lamb to a large platter.

Reduce the heat to medium-low. Add the onion, garlic, ginger, cumin, coriander, caraway, and red pepper flakes and cook for 5 minutes to toast the spices. Add the tomato paste and 2 cups of the chicken broth and stir well.

Return the lamb to the pot, increase the heat to medium, cover, and cook for about 1 hour, or until the lamb is fork-tender.

Add the remaining 2 cups broth and bring to a boil. Turn off the heat, stir in the spinach and bulgur, cover, and let stand for 15 minutes. Taste and adjust the seasoning.

To serve, ladle the stew into a large serving bowl or warmed shallow bowls. Serve with soup spoons and lots of warm pita breads.

SHOULDER LAMB CHOPS WITH SAFFRON BASMATI RICE AND WARMED TOMATOES

What I love about this recipe is that the pot is never wiped clean, leaving the juices of each component to impart their flavor. It's a true one-pot meal, where the lamb chops, rice, and sauce are all reheated together in the same pot, then scooped out onto a platter to serve. A bottle of Zinfandel would be perfect with this dish.

SERVING SUGGESTION: A simple coleslaw would be a lovely addition.

1 tablespoon sweet paprika
1 tablespoon salt, plus 1 teaspoon
4 double-cut lamb chops (about 7 ounces each)
2 tablespoons olive oil
2 ¾ cups chicken broth or water

2 cups cherry tomatoes, stemmed and halved
2 cloves garlic, minced
1 tablespoon minced fresh rosemary
½ cup minced fresh basil, plus basil leaves for garnish
2 tablespoons red wine vinegar

4 to 5 saffron threads
1 cup brown basmati rice
2 green onions, including green parts, thinly sliced

SERVES 4

In a large, shallow bowl, stir together the paprika and 1 tablespoon salt. Add the lamb chops and thoroughly coat.

In a large skillet, heat the olive oil over medium heat and brown the lamb chops for 5 minutes on each side.

Add 1 cup of the chicken broth, bring to a boil, reduce the heat to medium, and simmer for 20 minutes, turning the lamb occasionally.

Add the tomatoes, garlic, rosemary, minced basil, and vinegar to the skillet and continue to simmer for another 10 minutes.

Transfer the lamb chops and sauce to a large platter. Cover with aluminum foil to keep warm.

Meanwhile, make the saffron rice: Using the same skillet, without wiping it out add the remaining 1¾ cups broth, bring to a boil over high heat, then reduce to a simmer. Stir in the saffron, rice, green onions, and the 1 teaspoon salt. Cover and cook for about 20 minutes, or until the rice is tender. Use a fork to fluff the rice.

If the lamb chops and sauce are cold, put them back in the skillet, cover, and warm for about 5 minutes over low heat.

To serve, scoop the lamb chops and sauce onto the rice on a large platter or warmed plates. Garnish with basil leaves.

* * *

Lamb Meatballs with Steamed Kale over Linguine

This dish, a twist on spaghetti with meatballs, was created one spring when I was confronted with an overabundance of kale in my garden. Two bunches of kale might seem like too much, but you'll be surprised to see, as I was, that once it's cooked, it's just the right amount.

The lamb meatballs were inspired by my mom, who often substituted ground lamb in recipes that called for ground beef. These days, I actually prefer lamb meatballs over the more common beef rendition.

variations: To save time, instead of making meatballs, crumble the beef in the pan to make a more traditional Bolognese sauce. Instead of pasta, this lamb dish could be served over couscous or rice.

1 pound dried whole-wheat or egg linguine
2 bunches kale, coarsely chopped
1 pound ground lamb
2 shallots, minced
½ cup dried bread crumbs

1 tablespoon minced fresh rosemary
Salt and freshly ground pepper to taste
2 slices bacon, finely diced
¼ cup extra-virgin olive oil, plus more
   if desired

2 to 3 cloves garlic, minced
3 tablespoons minced fresh oregano
1 cup (4 ounces) grated Parmesan cheese
Red pepper flakes to taste (optional)

SERVES 6

In a large pasta pot, cook the pasta in salted boiling water until almost al dente, about 8 minutes. Add the kale to the pot and cook for 3 to 5 minutes, or until the pasta is al dente. Be sure not to overcook the pasta, because it will be reheated later.

While the pasta is cooking, in a medium bowl, combine the lamb, shallots, bread crumbs, and rosemary. Season with salt and pepper and set aside.

Drain the pasta and kale and run it under cold water to cool. Transfer it to a bowl and cover loosely with a towel.

Rinse out the pasta pot and set it over medium-high heat. Add the bacon and cook until crisp, about 4 minutes on each side. Using a slotted metal spatula, transfer the bacon to paper towels to drain. Dice the bacon and add it to the lamb mixture and combine well. Form the meat into 10 or 12 balls 1½ inches in diameter. Add the meatballs, in batches, to the pot and cook over medium-high heat, turning occasionally, until browned on all sides, 6 to 8 minutes.

Return the pasta and kale to the pot with the meatballs. Add the ¼ cup olive oil, the garlic, and oregano and reheat for 5 minutes over low heat. Add another tablespoon of olive oil at this time, if you like.

Add ¾ cup of the Parmesan cheese and, if you like, the red pepper flakes. Toss to combine thoroughly.

To serve, using tongs, transfer the linguine to a large platter or warmed plates. Arrange the meatballs and kale on top and garnish with the remaining Parmesan.

LAMB STROGANOFF WITH EGG NOODLES

Stroganoff is a classic dish in which the meat is browned, then cooked until meltingly tender, and finally ladled over broad egg noodles that soak up all the flavor. Though it's usually made with beef, I find the combination of sour cream and braised lamb irresistible. Once you try it, you won't want to go back to the other version.

VARIATION: Stroganoff is also delicious served over steamed vegetables or toasted slices of bread.

8 to 12 ounces dried broad egg noodles
2 tablespoons olive oil
2 tablespoons minced fresh flat-leaf parsley, plus more for garnish
1½ pounds lamb stew meat, cut into 1-inch chunks

Salt and freshly ground pepper to taste
1 onion, coarsely chopped
2 tablespoons tomato paste
1 teaspoon Dijon mustard
1 tablespoon sweet paprika
1 tablespoon Worcestershire sauce

8 ounces button mushrooms, thinly sliced
2 cups chicken broth
2 tablespoons all-purpose flour
1 cup sour cream

SERVES 4

In a large pasta pot of salted boiling water, cook the noodles until al dente, 8 to 10 minutes. Drain in a colander and rinse under cold water to cool. Put the noodles in a large bowl and toss with 1 tablespoon of the olive oil and the 2 tablespoons parsley. Set aside.

In the same pot, heat the remaining 1 tablespoon of olive oil over medium heat.

Season the lamb with salt and pepper and brown on all sides in the olive oil, about 10 minutes. Using a slotted spoon, transfer the lamb to a large platter.

In the same pot, cook the onion over medium heat for about 5 minutes, or until golden brown. Add the tomato paste, mustard, paprika, Worcestershire sauce, mushrooms, and 1½ cups of the chicken broth. Return the lamb to the pot, bring to a boil, then reduce the heat to low and simmer, uncovered, for about 1 hour, or until the lamb is fork-tender.

In a small bowl, whisk together the flour and the remaining ½ cup chicken broth. Stir the flour mixture into the simmering pot and cook for about 5 minutes, or until the sauce thickens slightly.

Just before serving, remove from heat and stir in the sour cream and salt and pepper to taste. Return the noodles to the pot, or transfer the Stroganoff to a serving dish, rinse out the pot, add a little warm water, and reheat the noodles over medium heat.

Serve the mixed noodles and Stroganoff on a large platter, or serve the noodles on a platter and spoon the Stroganoff over. Garnish with parsley.

RACK OF LAMB WITH TRUFFLED NEW POTATOES, ASPARAGUS, AND GREEN GARLIC

With one-pot cooking, we often think of heavy braises or slow-cooked stews. However, as this and a handful of other recipes in this book prove, some one-pot meals take less time, with far more eloquent results. This rack of lamb served on top of decadently truffled potatoes is elegant and relatively quick to prepare. Make this dish in springtime, when lamb is at its best, and asparagus and young garlic are fresh. If you can't find green garlic, substitute 2 green onions and 1 minced garlic clove.

Although rack of lamb is typically prepared in the oven, in this version the lamb is browned on the stove top in the same pot used to sauté the vegetables. Then all you have to do is reheat the lamb directly on top of the potatoes, asparagus, and green garlic. Talk about an easy, classy entertaining dish.

variation: Instead of adding the asparagus to the potatoes, cook it for a few minutes at the end and serve it as a side dish.

2 ½ pounds rack of lamb, frenched and cut into 4 equal pieces
3 cloves garlic, minced
Salt and freshly ground pepper to taste
¼ cup Dijon mustard
¼ cup honey

1 tablespoon minced fresh rosemary
4 tablespoons olive oil
2 to 3 stalks green garlic, thinly sliced
1½ pounds small new or fingerling potatoes, left whole or cut into bite-sized pieces
1 cup chicken broth

2 tablespoons black truffle oil
2 tablespoons unsalted butter
3 tablespoons minced fresh flat-leaf parsley
1 pound asparagus, trimmed and cut into 1-inch pieces

SERVES 4

Rub the lamb with the minced garlic and season with salt and pepper. In a small bowl, combine the mustard, honey, rosemary, and 1 tablespoon of the olive oil.

In a large, heavy skillet or shallow pot, heat 2 tablespoons of the olive oil over medium-high heat. Place the lamb racks in the pan, fat side down, and cook for 3 to 5 minutes, turning halfway through, until the meat is browned on both sides. Continue to cook, uncovered, for about 30 minutes or until an instant-read thermometer inserted in the center of the meat reads 120°F. At this point, it is better to undercook the lamb, because you will be rewarming it later. Transfer the lamb to a platter. Let the lamb cool slightly, then using a small spoon or brush, coat all sides of the lamb with the mustard mixture, reserving the remaining mixture.

In the same skillet, heat the remaining 1 tablespoon olive oil over medium heat, add the green garlic, and sauté for 2 minutes to just soften it.

Add the potatoes, chicken broth, and salt and pepper to taste to the skillet. Cover and simmer for about 15 minutes, or until the potatoes are very tender. Add the truffle oil, butter, and parsley.

Add the asparagus to the potatoes and gently toss to mix. Put the lamb racks on top. Reduce the heat to medium-low. Cover and warm for about 5 minutes to reheat but not overcook the lamb. Taste and adjust the seasoning.

To serve, transfer the lamb to a large platter or warmed individual plates. Spoon the vegetables alongside. Drizzle the remaining mustard sauce on top of lamb.

LaMB BURGERS WITH ORECCHIETTE, GORGONZOLA, and Pancetta

This is an adult rendition of burgers with mac 'n' cheese. Orecchiete is an ear-shaped pasta that will scoop up the Gorgonzola cream sauce and bits of salty pancetta. If you can't find orecchiette, elbow macaroni will work fine.

VARIATION AND SERVING SUGGESTION: Instead of burgers, form the lamb into 2-inch meatballs. Serve this dish with a side of steamed spinach (cooked ahead of time or at the last minute in the pot).

LaMB BURGERS

1½ pounds ground lamb

1 small red onion, shredded

1 tablespoon minced fresh rosemary

2 tablespoons minced fresh flat-leaf parsley

1 teaspoon salt

½ teaspoon freshly ground black pepper

1 tablespoon vegetable oil

4 ounces pancetta, cut into small strips

1 clove garlic, minced

12 ounces dried orecchiette pasta

1½ cups heavy cream

6 ounces Gorgonzola cheese, crumbled (about 1¼ cups)

½ cup (2 ounces) grated Asiago cheese

1 tablespoon minced fresh thyme

1 teaspoon finely ground white pepper

¼ teaspoon ground nutmeg

2 tablespoons minced fresh flat-leaf parsley for garnish

Salt to taste

SERVES 4

To make the lamb burgers: In a medium bowl, combine the lamb, onion, rosemary, parsley, salt, and pepper. Mix well. Using your hands, form the mixture into 4 patties about 3 inches in diameter and ¾ inch thick.

In a large skillet, heat the oil over medium-high heat, and cook the burgers 4 to 5 minutes on each side for medium-rare. Transfer to a plate.

Pour off the fat from the skillet. Add the pancetta and garlic and cook over medium heat for about 5 minutes, or until the pancetta is golden. Using a spatula, scrape everything out of the pan into a small bowl.

Fill the skillet about three-fourths full of water, add salt, and bring to a boil. Add the orecchiette and cook for about 12 minutes, or until al dente. Drain the pasta and return it to the skillet over medium-low heat. Add the cream, Gorgonzola, Asiago, thyme, pepper, and nutmeg. Bring to a simmer and cook for a few minutes until the sauce thickens slightly. Add the pancetta and juices and stir, cooking a few minutes longer.

Place the burgers directly on top of the orecchiette, cover, and cook for about 5 minutes, or long enough to rewarm the burgers.

To serve, scoop a big spoonful of orecchiette onto each of 4 warmed plates and place a lamb burger on top. Garnish with a generous sprinkling of parsley.

STOVE-TOP MOUSSAKA

This is a wonderful example of a dish that is typically cooked in the oven but can also be cooked in a pot on the stove. Compared to a traditional oven-baked moussaka, which requires a laborious layering of fried eggplant, lamb, and béchamel sauce and can take up to an hour to cook, this one-pot version is a snap. In this recipe, you make the béchamel sauce in the same pot as the moussaka; however, you can also make it in a separate saucepan.

SERVING SUGGESTION: A Greek salad of cucumbers, tomato, red onion, and feta drizzled with olive oil and a little vinegar would be a great complement to this one-pot dish.

BÉCHAMEL SAUCE
3 tablespoons unsalted butter
3 tablespoons all-purpose flour
2 egg yolks
1½ cups milk
¼ teaspoon ground nutmeg
Salt and freshly ground pepper to taste

1 eggplant, peeled and cut into ½-inch-thick crosswise slices
Salt for sprinkling, plus more to taste
2 tablespoons olive oil
1 pound ground lamb
1 onion, finely chopped
2 cloves garlic, minced

2 tablespoons minced fresh oregano
2 tomatoes, seeded and coarsely chopped
Freshly ground pepper to taste
3 ounces feta cheese, crumbled (about ⅔ cup)
2 tablespoons minced fresh flat-leaf parsley

SERVES 6

To make the béchamel sauce: In a large, heavy pot, melt the butter over medium heat. Whisk in the flour and cook, stirring constantly, until golden.

In a small bowl, stir together the egg yolks and milk. Gradually whisk the milk mixture into the flour mixture and simmer over low heat, whisking constantly, for about 5 minutes, or until it thickens slightly. Add the nutmeg and salt and pepper to taste. Scoop the sauce into a small bowl and press plastic wrap directly onto the surface of the sauce. Rinse the pot and set aside.

Cut the eggplant slices into ½-inch-wide strips. Salt lightly and place in a colander over the sink for at least 15 minutes.

Meanwhile, in the same pot, heat the olive oil over medium-high heat. Crumble the ground lamb into the pot, add the onion, and cook for about 5 minutes, stirring frequently, until the meat is brown all over.

Rinse off the eggplant, cut it into cubes, and add it to the pot. Cook, stirring occasionally, for 20 to 30 minutes, or until soft. Add the garlic, oregano, and tomatoes and cook for another 10 minutes, or until everything is soft and juicy. Season with salt and pepper to taste.

Reduce the heat to low. Using the back of a large spoon, gently push the lamb and eggplant mixture into the pot and smooth the top. Spoon the béchamel sauce on top and smooth with the back of the spoon. Sprinkle with the feta cheese and parsley.

Cover and cook for about 15 minutes, or until the sauce is heated through. Remove the pot from the heat and let sit for 5 minutes.

To serve, spoon into warmed shallow bowls. Don't worry about the way it looks; it will taste great.

POULTRY

nana's stewed chicken with summer squash

When my Nana's garden was overflowing with organic summer squash, she made this slow-cooked dish. I fondly remember having a bowl set before me with a big spoon and being encouraged to eat all of the juices, not wasting a bit. I tried never to let my Nana down.

variation: Add a few cut-up potatoes and a little broth when you add the squash and onions.

1 tablespoon chili powder

3 tablespoons dried Italian herbs

1 teaspoon salt, plus more to taste

½ teaspoon freshly ground pepper, plus more to taste

One 3- to 3½-pound chicken, cut into 8 serving pieces

3 tablespoons olive oil

1 onion, thinly sliced

2 pounds summer squash, such as zucchini, crooknecks, and/or pattypans, cut into 1½-inch pieces

4 cloves garlic, minced

¼ cup minced fresh oregano

1½ cups chicken broth

½ cup chopped fresh basil

One 4-ounce piece pecorino cheese

SERVES 4 TO 6

In a small bowl, combine the chili powder, herbs, the 1 teaspoon of salt, and the ½ teaspoon pepper. Rinse the chicken pieces and pat dry with paper towels, then toss with the spiced mixture to season generously all over.

In a large, heavy pot, heat the olive oil over medium heat. Add the chicken and cook, turning frequently, until browned on all sides, about 10 minutes. Using tongs, transfer the chicken to a platter.

Add the onion, squash, garlic, and oregano to the pot and cook for 5 minutes, or until slightly soft. Return the chicken to the pot, add the broth, and bring to a boil. Reduce the heat to medium-low, cover, and simmer, stirring occasionally, for about 45 minutes, or until the chicken is fork-tender. Stir in the basil and season with salt and pepper to taste.

To serve, spoon the chicken, vegetables, and juices onto a large platter or warmed plates. Using a vegetable peeler, shave the pecorino on top.

Chicken Wing Cacciatore with Creamy Polenta

My Italian grandmother always used to serve me chicken cacciatore spooned over creamy polenta. In this rendition, I use chicken wings, which are extremely flavorful, especially when they are braised, as they are here, until the meat literally falls off the bone.

Instead of being cooked separately, the polenta is added to the pot during the last half hour of cooking. To gild the lily, just before serving, I like to add a generous serving of butter and grated Parmesan cheese, which makes the dish even richer.

variation: For a complete meal, during the last 5 to 10 minutes of cooking time, add a few handfuls of green beans, cauliflower florets, corn kernels, or chopped chard.

2 to 3 pounds chicken wings
Salt and freshly ground pepper to taste
2 tablespoons olive oil
1 onion, coarsely chopped
2 cloves garlic, minced
1 red bell pepper, seeded and coarsely
   chopped

4 ounces button mushrooms, thinly sliced
2 large, very ripe tomatoes, seeded and
   chopped, or one 14-ounce can chopped
   organic tomatoes
1½ cups dry red wine
1 cup chopped fresh basil
2½ cups chicken broth

½ cup polenta
2 tablespoons minced fresh oregano
Freshly grated Parmesan cheese for garnish

SERVES 4

Rinse the chicken wings under cold running water and pat dry with paper towels. Using a sharp knife, cut off the pointed tips of the wings at the joint and discard. Generously salt and pepper the wings.

In a large, heavy pot, heat the olive oil over medium heat. Add the chicken wings and cook, uncovered and in batches, turning occasionally, until browned on all sides, about 15 minutes. Add the onion, garlic, bell pepper, mushrooms, tomatoes, red wine, ½ cup of the basil, and 1 cup of the broth. Bring to a boil, then reduce the heat to medium-low and simmer, stirring occasionally, for about 45 minutes, or until the meat is falling off the bone. The sauce will be slightly thickened.

Stir in the remaining broth and return to a boil. Reduce the heat to medium-low, stir in the polenta, and cook over medium-low heat for another 20 minutes, stirring frequently, until the polenta has thickened. Stir in the remaining ½ cup basil and the oregano and turn off the heat.

To serve, spoon the chicken wings and polenta onto a large platter or into warmed bowls, and set out plenty of napkins! Sprinkle with Parmesan cheese.

MOROCCAN CHICKEN WITH COUSCOUS

The inspiration for this dish came from a trip to Morocco with Oldways Preservation and Exchange Trust, a nonprofit organization that takes chefs, scientists, and writers around the world to study how ancient cuisines can promote modern health and happiness.

While soaking in the culture and filling myself with exotic food, I began to learn how to infuse the unique spices of North Africa into my American style of cooking. In Morocco, this one-pot dish would be cooked in a clay vessel called a tagine, and the couscous and stew would be cooked separately. However, in this recipe the couscous is cooked in the pot just before serving, creating a juicy side dish that's soaked up all the aromatic Moroccan spices. Don't worry if you have lots of leftovers; this tagine is even better the next day.

VARIATION AND SERVING SUGGESTION: Substitute lamb for the chicken. Serve with steamed greens for a more complete meal.

½ cup all-purpose flour

3 tablespoons sweet paprika

2 teaspoons salt, plus more to taste

½ teaspoon freshly ground pepper, plus more to taste

One 3- to 3½-pound chicken, cut into 8 serving pieces

2 to 3 tablespoons olive oil

1 yam or sweet potato, peeled and cut into 1-inch pieces

1 onion, thinly sliced

2 cloves garlic, minced

1 bay leaf

1 tablespoon ground cumin

1 tablespoon ground cardamom

1 teaspoon ground cinnamon

Generous pinch of saffron threads

½ cup raisins

½ cup chopped dried apricots

3 cups chicken broth

1 cup couscous

¼ cup minced fresh mint

SERVES 6

In a large bowl, combine the flour, paprika, the 2 teaspoons salt, and the ½ teaspoon pepper. Add the chicken and toss well to generously season on all sides.

In a large, heavy pot, heat the olive oil over medium-low heat. Add the chicken in batches and cook, turning occasionally, until brown on all sides, about 10 minutes.

≫ ≫ ≫ ≫

Add the yam, onion, garlic, bay leaf, cumin, cardamom, cinnamon, saffron, raisins, dried apricots, and chicken broth. Bring to a boil, then reduce the heat to medium-low, cover, and simmer for 1 hour, or until chicken is tender and the potatoes are very soft. Taste and adjust the seasoning.

Uncover, add the couscous and mint, and stir. Reduce the heat to low. Cover again and simmer for another 5 minutes. Turn off the heat and allow the pot to sit, covered, for 10 minutes. Uncover and, using tongs or a big fork, fluff everything in the pot. Put the lid back on and let sit for another 3 minutes.

To serve, scoop the couscous and chicken into a large serving bowl or warmed individual bowls. Serve with forks and big spoons for the couscous.

DUCK BREAST WITH CHERRIES AND WILD RICE PILAF

This delectable dish takes full advantage of the basic tenets of one-pot cooking but is quick to prepare and elegant enough to serve at a dinner party. The combination of sweet, hot, and salty flavors makes this a completely satisfying entrée. You can substitute rehydrated dried cherries when fresh cherries aren't in season.

VARIATION: For a more complete meal, during the last 10 minutes of cooking the rice, mix in about 1½ cups of finely shredded napa cabbage.

4 boneless duck breasts (about 24 ounces total)

Salt to taste, plus 1 teaspoon

Freshly ground pepper to taste

1 large leek, including light green parts, rinsed and thinly sliced

1 teaspoon minced jalapeño chili, or to taste

1 cinnamon stick, broken into 4 pieces

⅛ teaspoon ground nutmeg

2 tablespoons packed brown sugar

½ cup ruby port

1½ cups chicken broth

8 ounces pitted Bing cherries (about 1½ cups) or 4 ounces dried cherries, soaked in hot water for 15 minutes and drained

½ cup coarsely chopped pitted kalamata olives

2 tablespoons capers

¾ cup wild rice

½ cup chopped cashews

SERVES 4

Using a sharp knife, score the skin and fat (but not the meat) of the duck breasts at ½-inch intervals in a cross-hatch pattern. Season with salt and pepper to taste.

Place the duck breasts, fat side down, in a large, heavy skillet and cook over medium-low heat for about 8 minutes to brown the skin and release most of the fat. Turn the breasts over and cook for a minute or so to brown slightly. (Do not overcook; they will be reheated just before serving.) Transfer to a large platter and set aside.

≫ ≫ ≫ ≫

Pour off all but about 2 tablespoons of the duck fat. Add the leek and cook over medium-low heat for 2 minutes, or until slightly softened. Add the jalapeño chili, cinnamon, nutmeg, brown sugar, port, broth, and cherries and stir well. Bring to a boil, then reduce the heat to medium-low and simmer for 5 minutes, or until the sauce thickens slightly.

Add the olives, capers, rice, cashews, and the 1 teaspoon salt. Cover and simmer for about 20 minutes, or until the rice is cooked and most of the liquid is absorbed.

Just before serving, return the duck breasts to the skillet, placing them directly on top of the pilaf, cover and cook over low heat for about 2 minutes, or just long enough to warm them through.

To serve, arrange the duck breasts on a large platter or on warmed plates and surround with the rice pilaf.

CHICKEN THIGHS PUTTANESCA

Chicken thighs are great for one-pot cooking, because they stay moist when cooked for a long time. For a low-carb meal, serve this dish without the pasta and with a big Caesar salad. I like to make a double batch, because the leftovers are great the next morning served over eggs, with lots of toast to sop up the spicy puttanesca sauce.

variation: Skip the pasta and serve the puttanesca with pieces of warm crusty bread.

1 pound dried linguine

3 tablespoons olive oil

Salt to taste

4 large or 8 small chicken thighs

2 large, juicy tomatoes, seeded and chopped, or one 14-ounce can chopped tomatoes

2 to 3 cloves garlic, minced

½ cup coarsely chopped pitted kalamata olives

One 2-ounce can anchovies

2 tablespoons sugar

½ to 1 teaspoon red pepper flakes, or one minced fresh chili

2 tablespoons minced fresh oregano

2 tablespoons minced fresh flat-leaf parsley

¼ cup capers, drained

1 cup chopped fresh basil

Freshly ground pepper to taste

1 cup (4 ounces) grated Parmesan cheese for garnish

SERVES 4 GENEROUSLY

In a large, heavy pot, cook the pasta in salted boiling water until al dente, about 11 minutes. Drain, then rinse under cold water. Toss with 1 tablespoon of olive oil and a little salt in a large bowl.

In the same pot, heat the remaining 2 tablespoons olive oil over medium heat. Cook the chicken in batches, turning occasionally, for about 10 minutes, or until browned on both sides. Stir in the tomatoes, garlic, olives, anchovies, sugar, pepper flakes, oregano, parsley, capers, and ½ cup of the basil. Reduce the heat to low and simmer, stirring occasionally, for 30 minutes, or until the sauce has begun to thicken. Stir in the remaining basil and season with salt and pepper to taste.

To serve, divide the pasta among warmed bowls and ladle the chicken and sauce over. Garnish with the Parmesan cheese.

OLD-Fashioned Chicken Noodle Soup

The backbone to a good soup is the depth of the broth's flavor. Often, bones are used to make the broth, but in this recipe I use a whole chicken to give the broth a richer flavor. You can make your own homemade chicken stock by doubling this recipe and freezing the extra liquid in small portions in self-sealing plastic bags or ice-cube trays. Part of the meat can be used in this soup, and the rest can be used for sandwiches, chicken salad, or served on a bed of greens.

VARIATION: I often skip the noodles, to make a low-calorie, low-carb chicken soup.

8 ounces dried broad egg noodles
Olive oil for tossing (optional)
One 2 ½- to 3 ½-pound chicken, cut into
    eight pieces
1 large onion, coarsely chopped
2 carrots, peeled and coarsely chopped

2 stalks celery or fennel, coarsely chopped
1 bay leaf
3 thyme sprigs
3 dill sprigs
5 black peppercorns

2 cups assorted seasonal vegetables, such
    as green peas, corn kernels, or chopped
    bok choy, spinach, kale, or green beans
Salt and freshly ground pepper to taste

SERVES 6

If you prefer a clear soup, cook the noodles ahead of time in a large pot of salted boiling water until tender, about 10 minutes. Drain in a colander and rinse under cold water. Place the noodles in a large bowl, toss with a little olive oil, and set aside or refrigerate until ready to use.

In a very large, heavy pot, combine the chicken, onion, carrots, celery, bay leaf, thyme, dill, and peppercorns. (If you want a deeper, nuttier flavor for your soup, brown the chicken parts first in a little oil.)

≫ ≫ ≫ ≫

Add enough cold water to generously cover the chicken and vegetables and bring to a boil over high heat. Immediately reduce the heat to low and simmer, covered, for at least 2 hours, or until the broth tastes rich and full. Be sure that the broth doesn't come to a rolling boil, or it might become cloudy.

Strain the broth through a colander set over a large bowl and set aside to cool. If you want to remove the fat, refrigerate the broth until the fat rises to the top and congeals, then remove it.

Pick the chicken meat from the bones and return it to the pot along with 6 to 8 cups of the broth. If you haven't already cooked the noodles, add the noodles and seasonal vegetables and simmer for about 10 minutes, or until the noodles and vegetables are tender. If you have already cooked the noodles, return them to the pot for a brief time to warm, about 2 minutes. Season with salt and pepper.

To serve, ladle into warmed bowls.

SLOW-COOKED CHICKEN IN A POT

A whole chicken slow-cooked on the stove top until the meat falls off the bone is one of my all-time favorite one-pot meals. Because the chicken is braised, the meat remains moist and succulent, while absorbing whatever flavors you add to the pot. Plus, you end up with a nourishing broth to serve alongside.

This recipe is intentionally basic and Italian-style, leaving room to personalize by adding your favorite fresh herbs, veggies, or spices. Whatever you choose, I strongly advise that you use an organic chicken if possible, which is likely to have an abundance of flavor. A good-quality local or free-range chicken will result in a rich taste.

VARIATION: It may not present as nicely, but instead of using a whole chicken, precut chicken parts work just as well and can be easier to handle.

One 3- to 3½-pound chicken, organic and free-range if possible
Salt and freshly ground pepper to taste
1 lemon, quartered
3 rosemary sprigs
2 tablespoons vegetable oil, optional
1 onion, coarsely chopped
2 carrots, peeled and coarsely chopped
1 to 2 stalks celery, cut into 1-inch slices
12 ounces potatoes, peeled and cut into 1½-inch pieces
1 bay leaf
5 black peppercorns, crushed

10 fresh flat-leaf Italian parsley sprigs
1½ cups chicken broth

Suggestions for seasonings to be added halfway through:

ASIAN
2 tablespoons minced fresh ginger
3 tablespoons soy sauce
2 cloves garlic, minced

ITALIAN
½ cup chopped fresh basil
2 tablespoons minced fresh oregano
1 tomato, chopped

MEXICAN
½ cup chopped fresh cilantro
1 tablespoon ground cumin
2 cloves garlic, minced
1 jalapeño chili, finely chopped

BARBECUE
¼ cup packed brown sugar
2 tablespoons vinegar
2 tablespoons Dijon mustard
1 teaspoon dried chipotle powder

SERVES 4 TO 6

Rinse the chicken under cold running water and pat dry with paper towels. Using a sharp knife, trim off any excess fat.

≫ ≫ ≫ ≫

Generously season the chicken inside and out with salt and pepper. Put the lemon pieces inside the cavity of the chicken along with the rosemary. At this time, if you choose to, heat the oil over medium-high heat and brown the chicken on all sides, about 7 to 10 minutes. Transfer the chicken to a platter.

In a large, heavy pot, combine the onion, carrots, celery, potatoes, bay leaf, peppercorns, and parsley sprigs. Pour the broth over the vegetables and season with salt and pepper to taste.

Place the chicken on top of the vegetables. Bring the liquid to a boil, then reduce the heat to low, cover, and simmer for about 1½ hours, or until the meat nearly falls off the bone. While cooking, baste the chicken occasionally with the juices. This is also the opportunity to sign this dish with one of the variations given, or with your own personal flavors.

When the chicken is done, using two large forks or tongs, transfer it to a cutting board and either cut into serving-size pieces or carve as you would a turkey. Transfer to a platter using a slotted spoon, remove the vegetables, and arrange them on the platter next to the chicken.

Increase the heat to high and reduce the juices until you have about 1 cup to use as an au jus sauce. Taste and adjust the seasoning. Pour the juices through a sieve over the chicken and vegetables and serve.

TURKEY MEATBALLS WITH PASTINA

This is a great dish to make for kids. They'll love the tiny rice-shaped pasta. This is a perfect opportunity to get your kids to help in the kitchen by mixing and shaping the meatballs. Ground beef or lamb can be substituted for turkey.

SERVING SUGGESTION: Serve with steamed or sautéed seasonal vegetables.

MEATBALLS

2 pounds ground turkey

1 onion, shredded

1 carrot, peeled and shredded

1 teaspoon ground sage

2 eggs, beaten

½ cup fresh bread crumbs

2 teaspoons salt

¼ teaspoon freshly ground pepper

¼ cup vegetable oil

2 cups firmly packed shredded red or green cabbage

2 cloves garlic, minced

2 cups chicken broth

1 cup pastina pasta

Salt to taste

¼ cup minced fresh flat-leaf parsley

Freshly ground pepper to taste

SERVES 6

To make the meatballs: In a large bowl, combine the turkey, onion, carrot, and sage. Stir in the eggs, bread crumbs, salt, and pepper. Using your hands, form the meat into balls about 1 inch in diameter. You should have 16 to 20 meatballs.

In a large, heavy pot, heat the oil over medium heat. Add the meatballs in batches and cook until brown on all sides, 6 to 7 minutes.

Add the cabbage and garlic. Cover and cook over low heat for 5 minutes, or until the cabbage is softened.

Add the chicken broth, bring to a boil, then reduce the heat to low, cover, and simmer for 10 minutes to cook the meatballs.

Increase the heat to high and bring the liquid to a boil. Add the pastina and a little salt. Stir well, reduce the heat to medium, and simmer, uncovered, for about 7 minutes, or until the pastina is al dente.

Just before serving, stir in the parsley and season with salt and pepper to taste.

To serve, spoon onto a big platter or onto warmed plates.

TURKEY FRICASSEE WITH STEAMED ASPARAGUS

This fricassee is based on an Early American stew finished with milk and flour to make a thick, comforting gravy. If you can't find a turkey thigh, use an equal weight of chicken thighs.

SERVING SUGGESTION: This dish is great spooned over thick slices of toasted bread for a comforting complete meal.

One 2-pound boneless turkey thigh
½ cup all-purpose flour
1½ teaspoons salt
½ teaspoon freshly ground pepper
1 tablespoon olive oil
1 onion, thinly sliced
1½ cups chicken broth

1 teaspoon sweet paprika
1 tablespoon minced fresh rosemary
½ cup fruity sweet white wine such as Gewürtzraminer or Riesling
1 cup milk
4 tablespoons unsalted butter

1 pound asparagus, trimmed and cut into 1½-inch pieces
1 cup chunky cranberry sauce

SERVES 6

Rinse the turkey under cold, running water, pat dry with paper towels, and place in a large bowl. Add ¼ cup of the flour, the salt, and the pepper. Toss to coat the meat completely. Shake off any excess flour.

In a large, heavy skillet, heat the olive oil over medium heat. Brown the turkey thigh on both sides, turning a few times, for about 10 minutes. Add the onion, broth, paprika, rosemary, and wine. Cover and simmer for about 2 hours, or until fork-tender. Using a large fork, transfer the turkey thigh to a cutting board.

Put the remaining ¼ cup flour in a medium bowl and gradually stir in the milk to make a smooth liquid.

Add the butter to the skillet and melt over medium heat. Add the flour mixture and whisk constantly until the sauce thickens slightly.

Just before serving, add the asparagus to the skillet. Put the turkey on top to rewarm. Cover and cook for about 5 minutes. Using tongs or a big fork, transfer the turkey to a cutting board and cut into ½-inch-thick slices.

To serve, spoon the asparagus and sauce onto a large platter or into warmed shallow bowls. Top with slices of turkey and a few tablespoons of cranberry sauce.

SHELLFISH AND FISH

STEAMED SCALLOPS WITH GREEN BEANS AND PURPLE POTATOES

Cooking an entire meal using stackable bamboo or metal steamer baskets that fit into your favorite wok or pot is a trick that I've picked up from Chinese cooking. This style of vertical cooking is the ultimate one-pot technique, in which you put the ingredients (such as the potatoes in this recipe), that require the longest cooking time on the bottom, nearest the steaming liquid, and those requiring the least time, such as scallops and green beans, on top. Have the baskets filled with whatever you are steaming before you begin. As with many of the recipes in this book, cooking in stages is a big part of the success of the dish. Steamer baskets are a great way to cook the various components to their optimum flavor and texture while keeping them separate.

Purple potatoes are available in most specialty grocery stores. The flesh becomes more intensely purple when cooked. You can also substitute any boiling potato, especially nutty-flavored golden fingerlings or new potatoes, which are also beautiful and delicious.

SERVING SUGGESTION: A salad, simply dressed with a light vinaigrette, would be perfect with this one-pot meal.

10 to 12 large flat-leaf parsley sprigs
5 cloves garlic, minced
3 to 5 large tarragon sprigs
Pinch of saffron threads
3 tablespoons olive oil

1 pound purple potatoes, cut into
    ¾-inch wedges
Salt and freshly ground pepper to taste
½ cup chopped fresh basil
1 tablespoon Dijon mustard
1 teaspoon curry powder

Juice of 1 large lemon
1½ pounds sea scallops
8 ounces green or yellow snap beans,
    trimmed and cut into 2-inch pieces

SERVES 4

Remove the leaves of 5 of the parsley sprigs, mince, and set aside in a small bowl.

Add 1 cup of water to a wok or a steamer pot, then add the remaining 5 sprigs parsley, half of the garlic, all the tarragon, saffron, and 1 tablespoon of the olive oil. Cover and bring to a simmer over medium-low heat.

In a medium bowl, combine the potatoes with 1 tablespoon of the olive oil and the remaining minced garlic, and season generously with salt and pepper. Place the potatoes in a bamboo or metal steamer basket and set snugly in the wok or pot above the simmering water. Cover and steam for 8 minutes, or until half-cooked.

Meanwhile, in a medium bowl, combine the remaining 1 tablespoon olive oil, the basil, mustard, curry powder, lemon juice, scallops, and beans. Season generously with salt and pepper.

Put the scallops and beans on top of the potatoes in a separate basket or directly on top of the potatoes in the same basket. Cover and cook until the potatoes are tender and the scallops are opaque and tender to the touch, 3 to 7 minutes, depending upon size.

To serve, remove the baskets from the wok or pot. Using tongs or a fork, remove everything from the baskets and arrange artfully on 4 warmed plates.

eDDIe's FISH and eGGS

When I was growing up, my family vacationed most summers in Atlantic City, staying in a little apartment a few blocks from the boardwalk. My dad, Eddie, an Orthodox Jew, did not eat pork, which means we found no bacon or ham on our breakfast table. However, nearly every morning, my dad would head for the fish market at 5 A.M. and return to prepare this dish long before we awakened. No one else I knew ate fish for breakfast. As an adult, I crave this breakfast, which my family still calls "Eddie's Fish and Eggs."

SERVING SUGGESTIONS: Serve this one-pot dish with buttered toast and a good shake of hot sauce.

⅓ cup all-purpose flour

½ cup grated Parmesan cheese

¾ teaspoon salt, plus more to taste

½ teaspoon freshly ground pepper, plus more to taste

1 pound white-fleshed fish fillets, such as cod, sole, flounder, or snapper

Vegetable oil for frying, plus 2 tablespoons

1 russet potato, cut into ½-inch dice

1 yellow onion, cut into ½-inch dice

½ green bell pepper, seeded and cut into ½-inch dice

¾ teaspoon sweet paprika

1 tablespoon minced fresh dill

10 eggs, beaten

2 green onions, including green parts, chopped, for garnish

Buttered toast, hot sauce, and catsup for serving (optional)

SERVES 4

In a medium bowl, combine the flour, ¼ cup of the Parmesan, the ¾ teaspoon salt, and ½ teaspoon of the pepper. Stir to blend. Add the fish and toss with the seasoned flour mixture.

In a large, heavy skillet, heat 1/16 inch oil over medium heat. Add the fish in batches and fry for about 5 minutes, or until lightly browned on all sides. As the pieces are cooked, transfer them to paper towels to drain.

Using a paper towel, wipe the skillet clean. Add the 2 tablespoons oil and heat over medium heat. Add the potato, onion, and bell pepper and cook, stirring frequently, for about 20 minutes, or until the potatoes are soft. Add the paprika and salt and pepper to taste.

Return the fish to the skillet, add the dill, and stir. Add the eggs and remaining grated cheese. Using a rubber spatula, move the mixture around, pushing the eggs from the outer edges inward to begin the cooking.

Reduce the heat to low, cover, and cook for 5 or 6 minutes, or until the eggs are firm in the center. Do not overcook; the eggs will keep cooking even after you take them off the heat.

To serve, use a large spoon or spatula to scoop out the fish and eggs onto a large platter or warmed plates. Sprinkle with the green onions. Serve with buttered toast, hot sauce, and catsup, if you like.

Salmon and Mussel Chowder with Fava Beans

Seafood chowder is one of oldest all-American examples of a hearty one-pot meal, in which shellfish, potatoes, and vegetables cook together, absorbing each other's flavors. Unlike New England chowder, this recipe calls for salmon and mussels instead of clams. Use wild salmon whenever possible, or use sustainably farmed fish if it isn't wild. You can also substitute a mild white fish, such as haddock, cod, or halibut, for the salmon.

Serving suggestion: Ladle the chowder over thick slices of toasted white bread.

1½ pounds fava beans, shelled
2 cups bottled clam juice
1½ pounds salmon, skin and pinbones
    removed, cut into 1-inch pieces
1 pound mussels, scrubbed and debearded
3 thick slices bacon, cut into ½-inch pieces
1 onion, finely chopped

1 stalk celery, cut into ¼-inch-thick slices
3 potatoes, cut into ½-inch dice
1 bay leaf
2 tablespoons tomato paste
2 cups heavy cream
2 cups whole milk
Pinch of cayenne pepper

Salt and freshly ground pepper to taste
1 tablespoon minced fresh chives
    for garnish

SERVES 6

Bring about 2 cups of water to boil in a large, heavy pot (you will be using the same pot for the chowder.) Cook the fava beans for 3 to 5 minutes, depending on size. Remove the beans and run under cold water. Using the tip of a knife, cut a small slit in the skin of each fava bean, then squeeze out the bean. Set the beans aside. Discard the water used for cooking the favas.

In the same pot, bring the clam juice to a boil, then reduce the heat to medium-low. Add the salmon and simmer for 3 minutes. Using a slotted spoon, transfer the salmon to a large bowl and set aside.

Add the mussels to the broth, cover, and simmer for about 5 minutes, or until they open. Discard any that do not open. Using a slotted spoon, transfer the mussels to the bowl with the salmon. Pour the broth through a fine-meshed sieve into a medium bowl and reserve.

Using a paper towel, wipe out the pot. Add the bacon, onion, and celery to the pot and cook over medium heat for 5 minutes, or until the bacon is lightly browned. Add the potatoes, bay leaf, tomato paste, and reserved broth. Bring to a boil, then reduce the heat to medium-low and simmer, uncovered, for 20 minutes, or until the potatoes are cooked half to three-fourths of the way through.

Add the cream, milk, and cayenne and stir. Return the salmon and mussels to the pot along with the fava beans and simmer for 5 minutes to warm through. Season with salt and pepper.

To serve, ladle the chowder into warmed deep soup bowls. Garnish with the chives.

LOBSTER BISQUE WITH POTATOES

This is by far the most expensive and laborious recipe in this book. However, it is worth both the money and time, because it is delicious and sensuous beyond words. In fact, we serve this bisque at my restaurants, without the potatoes, as a first course every Valentine's Day. We always make enough for the staff. At the end of the busiest night of the year, even with their choice of anything on the menu, they choose the bisque.

VARIATION: To transform this into a complete one-pot meal, add a handful of quick-cooking fresh or frozen vegetables, such as corn, beans, zucchini, or peas, during the last few minutes.

1 cup (2 sticks) unsalted butter
2 celery stalks, coarsely chopped
1 carrot, peeled and coarsely chopped
1 yellow onion, coarsely chopped
1 teaspoon sweet paprika
1 bay leaf
5 whole peppercorns

10 large flat-leaf parsley sprigs
One 28-ounce can chopped tomatoes
½ cup dry sherry
2 live lobsters, 1½ pounds each
⅓ cup all-purpose flour
2 golden-fleshed potatoes, such as Yukon
    Gold or fingerlings, cut into ½-inch pieces

2 cups heavy cream
Salt and freshly ground white pepper
    to taste
2 green onions, including green parts,
    finely chopped

SERVES 4 TO 6

In a very large, heavy pot, melt ¼ cup of the butter over medium heat and cook the celery, carrot, onion, and paprika for 5 minutes, or until the vegetables are soft. Add the bay leaf, peppercorns, parsley, tomatoes, and half the sherry. Simmer for 5 minutes.

Put the lobsters in the pot, add 2 cups of water, and cover. Cook for 15 minutes.

Using tongs, transfer the lobsters to a plate to let sit until cool to the touch.

Meanwhile, make a tomato broth by putting the contents of the pot through a medium-meshed sieve set over a medium-large bowl, pushing the solids through with the back of a large spoon.

Remove the meat from the lobsters and reserve the shells. Twist off the claws, crack gently with a hammer, and using a pick or small fork, remove the meat. Using a knife or scissors, cut through the shell on the bottom of the tail, pull apart, and remove the lobster meat. Set aside. Put the lobster shells in a food processor and pulse for 3 to 4 minutes.

Return the pot to the stove and melt ½ cup of the butter over medium heat. Add the lobster shells and remaining sherry and cook for 10 minutes. Empty the pot into a medium-meshed sieve set over a bowl and push the solids through with the back of a large spoon.

Return the pot to medium heat and melt the remaining ¼ cup butter. Whisk in the flour and cook, stirring constantly, for 3 to 4 minutes, or until the mixture turns a golden brown.

Add the tomato broth and potatoes to the stock and simmer, uncovered, for about 20 minutes, or until the potatoes are soft. Add the lobster butter and cream and cook for 5 minutes. Season with salt and pepper.

To serve, chop the lobster meat into ½-inch pieces and divide among 4 shallow bowls. Ladle the bisque and some potatoes into each bowl and garnish with the green onions.

FRIED RICE WITH MANGO, SHRIMP, AND EGG

When my boys were young, I tried to keep the refrigerator filled with home-cooked snacks. Mostly, I did it to get them to eat something reasonably nourishing at home. I was not a fascist about it, but I did try to steer them and their buddies away from fatty, sugary temptations. After a day of school, the hungry boys would come home and, instead of reaching for chips, they would open the refrigerator for made-from-scratch snacks, such as macaroni and cheese, burritos, nachos, organic fruit salad, or this fried rice.

Although you could make this dish in a wok, a large skillet is really all you need. This is a great way to use up all those cartons of leftover rice from take-out dinners. In fact, you don't want to use freshly cooked rice, because it will absorb too much of the oil.

SERVING SUGGESTION: A simple dessert of green tea ice cream would make this a perfect any-occasion meal.

4 tablespoons vegetable oil
6 eggs
2 cloves garlic, minced
1½ cups bean sprouts
1 yellow onion, thinly sliced

2 celery stalks, thinly sliced
2 tablespoons minced fresh ginger
3 green onions, including green parts, thinly sliced
One 8-ounce can sliced water chestnuts, drained

3 cups cold cooked white rice
12 ounces shrimp, shelled
1 cup mango, peeled and chopped into ¼-inch pieces
2 tablespoons soy sauce or to taste

SERVES 4 TO 6

In a large, heavy skillet, heat 2 tablespoons of the oil over medium heat. Crack the eggs into the pan and, using a fork, break the yolks. Fry for about 3 minutes on each side, or until the yolks are firm. Using a metal spatula, transfer the eggs to a cutting board and cut into bite-sized pieces.

Add the remaining 2 tablespoons oil to the skillet and cook the garlic, sprouts, onion, and celery for 3 minutes, or until softened. Stir in the ginger, green onions, water chestnuts, rice, shrimp, mango, and eggs.

Cover and cook for another 3 minutes, or until the rice begins to brown on the bottom. Add the 2 tablespoons soy sauce and, using a rubber spatula, toss the rice to brown. Taste and add more soy sauce if desired.

To serve, spoon the fried rice onto a large platter or into warmed shallow bowls.

SHRIMP WITH CORN ON THE COB and SUMMER Beans

This dish is in the spirit of a traditional New England crab boil. For me, sweet corn, shrimp, and fresh beans steamed together in a pot is the quintessential summer meal. Although it's a very homey dish, I love serving it at a casual dinner party. Simply put the pot in the middle of your table, forgo the forks, and invite your guests to dig in. Put out a big basket of hand towels and wedges of fresh lemon for cleansing hands.

SERVING SUGGESTIONS: Although this is a complete meal, a loaf of warm, crusty bread for sopping up the juices and a plate of sliced summer tomatoes and cucumbers sprinkled with basil and olive oil are great accompaniments.

1 tablespoon olive oil
5 shallots, minced
5 cloves garlic, thinly sliced
1 cup dry white wine
2 bay leaves

6 whole peppercorns
4 cups water
Salt and freshly ground pepper to taste
3 pounds large shrimp (16 to 20 per pound)
4 ears corn, shucked and broken in half

8 ounces green, yellow, and/or purple snap beans, trimmed and cut into 2-inch pieces
2 to 3 tablespoons unsalted butter

SERVES 4 TO 6

In a large, heavy pot, heat the olive oil over medium heat. Add the shallots and garlic and cook for 3 minutes, or until the shallots are soft. Add the wine, bay leaves, peppercorns, and water. Season with salt and pepper. Bring to a boil, then reduce the heat to medium-low and simmer, uncovered, for 5 minutes.

Add the shrimp, corn, and beans. Cover and simmer for 3 to 5 minutes, or until the shrimp are pink and just beginning to curl and the beans are crisp-tender. Stir in the butter.

To serve, transfer the pot to a trivet set on the table. Accompany with tongs and a ladle so your guests can serve themselves, along with bowls, spoons, and a loaf of warm, crusty bread for dipping.

MONKFISH WITH TOMATOES, ANCHOVIES, GREEN OLIVES, AND BASIL

This zesty Provencal-inspired stew showcases the sun-drenched ingredients of the Mediterranean summer, including monkfish, which is native to the region. The dish really shines when you use good cured olives. There are so many wonderful varieties available in specialty grocery stores. Go on an olive tasting!

Monkfish is called the poor man's lobster because of its mild, sweet flavor and tender texture. If you can find halibut cheeks, they would be a wonderful substitute for the monkfish.

VARIATION: For a complete meal, thicken the stew with rice: Just before putting the monkfish back in the pot, add an extra cup of water and ½ cup basmati rice to the tomato mixture.

1½ pounds monkfish fillets
½ cup all-purpose flour
Salt and freshly ground pepper to taste
3 tablespoons olive oil
2 cloves garlic, minced
One 2-ounce can anchovies, drained and
   coarsely chopped

2 very ripe tomatoes, seeded and coarsely
   chopped, or one 14-ounce can chopped
   tomatoes
2 tablespoons capers
½ cup olives, pitted and coarsely chopped
   (see note)
2 tablespoons sugar

2 tablespoons balsamic vinegar
1 cup water
½ cup minced fresh basil
1 to 1½ ounces grated aged goat cheese,
   such as manouri or goat gouda
½ teaspoon red pepper flakes

SERVES 4

Cut the monkfish into ½-inch-thick medallions. Put the flour in a medium bowl and season generously with salt and pepper. Add the monkfish and toss to coat.

In a large, heavy skillet, heat 1½ tablespoons of the olive oil over medium heat. Add the monkfish in batches and cook on each side for 2 to 3 minutes, or until lightly browned. Transfer the monkfish to a large platter.

Add the remaining 1½ tablespoons of the olive oil to the skillet along with the garlic, anchovies, tomatoes, capers, olives, sugar, and balsamic vinegar. Add the water, bring to a boil, then reduce the heat to low. Simmer, uncovered, for 15 minutes, or until the liquid thickens slightly. Stir in the basil, then season with salt and pepper to taste.

Return the monkfish to the skillet, pushing it into the sauce until submerged halfway. Cover and cook for 3 to 5 minutes, or until the monkfish is opaque throughout and fork-tender.

To serve, transfer the fish and sauce to a large platter or warmed plates. Spoon the sauce over and accompany with the goat cheese and pepper flakes.

PITTING OLIVES: Place a small handful of olives between a single fold of a clean dish towel. Using the side of a large chef's knife, push firmly on the towel until you feel the olives crush. Uncover and remove the pits with your hands.

Deviled Crab in a Pot

Deviled crab is usually baked in the oven. My mom used to bake it in little red ceramic crab molds. Sometimes I think this classic recipe is called "deviled" not because it is spicy but because it is devilishly good.

This is one of the few recipes in this book that calls for finishing the dish under the broiler, so you'll need to use an ovenproof pot.

SERVING SUGGESTION: To complete this meal, serve with a simple butter lettuce salad.

6 tablespoons unsalted butter
1 cup dried bread crumbs
1 teaspoon grated lemon zest
1¼ cups heavy cream or whole milk

2 eggs, beaten
½ teaspoon salt
1½ teaspoons dry mustard
¼ teaspoon cayenne pepper

1 pound fresh lump crabmeat, picked over
    for shell
6 to 8 thick wedges of country bread,
    toasted

SERVES 4 TO 6

Preheat the boiler. In a medium skillet or flameproof gratin dish, melt the butter over medium heat. Pour half the melted butter into a medium bowl and mix it with ½ cup of the bread crumbs. Cover and set aside.

Stir the remaining bread crumbs and the lemon zest into the butter already in the skillet. Whisk in the cream and cook over medium-low heat for 3 to 4 minutes, stirring often, until smooth. Remove from the heat and very gradually whisk in the beaten eggs, then the salt, mustard, and cayenne. Stir in the crabmeat and combine all the ingredients thoroughly.

Sprinkle the buttered crumbs on top to cover completely. Place under the broiler, about 4 to 6 inches from the heat source, for 2 to 3 minutes, or until the top is lightly browned.

Serve in the pot, surrounded by the wedges of toasted bread.

CORNMEAL-CRUSTED HALIBUT WITH TOMATO AND PEPPER STEW

The cornmeal crust on the fish makes a delicious, soft coating that absorbs the aromatic essence of the tomato and pepper stew. The combination of aroma, texture, and flavor is a feast for the senses.

SERVING SUGGESTION: Serve the fish over pasta cooked in the same pot either before or after you prepare the halibut.

½ cup cornmeal

2 tablespoons minced fresh thyme

1 tablespoon salt, plus more to taste

1 teaspoon sweet paprika

2 pounds halibut fillets

½ cup olive oil

3 cloves garlic, thinly sliced

1 onion, thinly sliced

1 red bell pepper, seeded and thinly sliced

1 large ripe tomato, seeded and coarsely chopped

¼ cup dry red wine

¼ teaspoon saffron threads (optional)

Freshly ground pepper to taste

5 tablespoons minced fresh flat-leaf parsley

SERVES 4

In a large bowl, stir the cornmeal, thyme, the 1 tablespoon salt, and the paprika together.

Rinse the halibut under cold running water. Pat dry and dredge fillets in the cornmeal mixture to coat both sides generously.

In a large, heavy skillet, heat ¼ cup of the olive oil over medium-high heat. Cook the fish, in batches, for about 4 minutes on each side, or until browned. Transfer the fish to a large platter and set aside.

Add the remaining ¼ cup olive oil and heat over medium heat. Add the garlic, onion, pepper, tomato, wine, and saffron. Reduce the heat, cover, and simmer for 30 minutes, or until the sauce has thickened slightly. Season with salt and pepper to taste, then stir in 3 tablespoons of the parsley.

Return the fish to the pot, placing it directly on top of the stew and spooning some of the stew over the fish. Cover and cook for 5 minutes to reheat the fish.

To serve, using a spatula or large spoon, transfer the fish to a serving platter or warmed plates. Smother with the sauce and garnish with the remaining parsley.

stove-top tuna noodle casserole

In this updated stove-top rendition of the homey tuna noodle casserole, you can use either fresh or canned tuna. Fresh tuna has a milder flavor and is a great way to use up leftover grilled tuna from a previous dinner. But truth be told, I prefer canned tuna for this recipe, which conjures up memories of my childhood.

variation: Canned salmon or steamed halibut or Atlantic cod could be substituted.

12 ounces dried broad egg noodles

2 tablespoons unsalted butter

½ onion, finely chopped

2 tablespoons all-purpose flour

2 cups whole milk

½ teaspoon dry mustard

1 teaspoon Worcestershire sauce

10 ounces tuna fillet, steamed, roasted, or grilled to well done, or two 6-ounce cans water-packed tuna, drained

½ cup fresh or frozen green peas

1½ cups (6 ounces) shredded cheddar cheese

Salt and freshly ground white pepper to taste

1 green onion, including green parts, finely chopped

1 tablespoon minced fresh flat-leaf parsley

SERVES 4

In a large, heavy pot of salted boiling water, cook the noodles until tender, 7 to 10 minutes. Drain in a colander and run under cold water. Transfer to a large bowl and set aside.

In the same pot, melt the butter over medium heat. Add the onion and cook for 2 minutes to soften.

Whisk in the flour and cook for 2 to 3 minutes, or until it bubbles. Gradually whisk in the milk. Add the mustard and Worcestershire sauce and cook, stirring constantly, for 1 minute, or until the mixture begins to simmer and thicken. Add the tuna, peas, and 1 cup of the cheese. Season with salt and pepper.

Add the cooked noodles, stir to combine thoroughly, and turn off the heat. Sprinkle the remaining ½ cup cheese and the green onion and parsley evenly on top. Cover and set aside for 5 minutes to melt the cheese.

To serve, put the pot on the table with a serving spoon and 4 bowls.

angel Hair Pasta with basil, chilies, and clams

Though you will usually find me at one of my restaurants, I still like to cook and eat at home. This recipe for angel hair pasta with clams is a favorite because it has simple flavors and comes together quickly. I like to cook the pasta ahead of time, then finish the sauce when I'm ready to eat.

serving suggestion: Serve with a side of steamed broccoli, cauliflower, or green beans.

12 ounces dried angel hair pasta
⅓ cup olive oil
3 cloves garlic, minced
2 very ripe tomatoes, seeded and coarsely chopped, or one 14-ounce can chopped tomatoes

1½ cups coarsely chopped fresh basil
½ cup dry white wine
2 tablespoons unsalted butter
½ teaspoon red chili flakes
3 pounds clams, rinsed

Salt and freshly ground pepper to taste
½ cup (2 ounces) grated Asiago cheese for garnish

SERVES 4

In a large, heavy pot of salted boiling water, cook the pasta until al dente, about 2 minutes. Drain in a colander and rinse the pasta under cold running water. Transfer the pasta to a large bowl, toss with 1 tablespoon of the olive oil, and set aside.

In the same pot, heat the remaining olive oil over medium heat. Add the garlic, tomatoes, and 1 cup of the basil and cook for 5 minutes. Add the wine, butter, chili flakes, and clams.

Cover, reduce the heat to low, and cook for 8 to 10 minutes, or until the clams fully open. Discard any clams that do not open. Return the pasta to the pot, stir to coat with the sauce, then season with salt and pepper.

To serve, using tongs, transfer the pasta to a large platter or warmed shallow bowls. Arrange the clams on top and garnish with the remaining basil and the cheese.

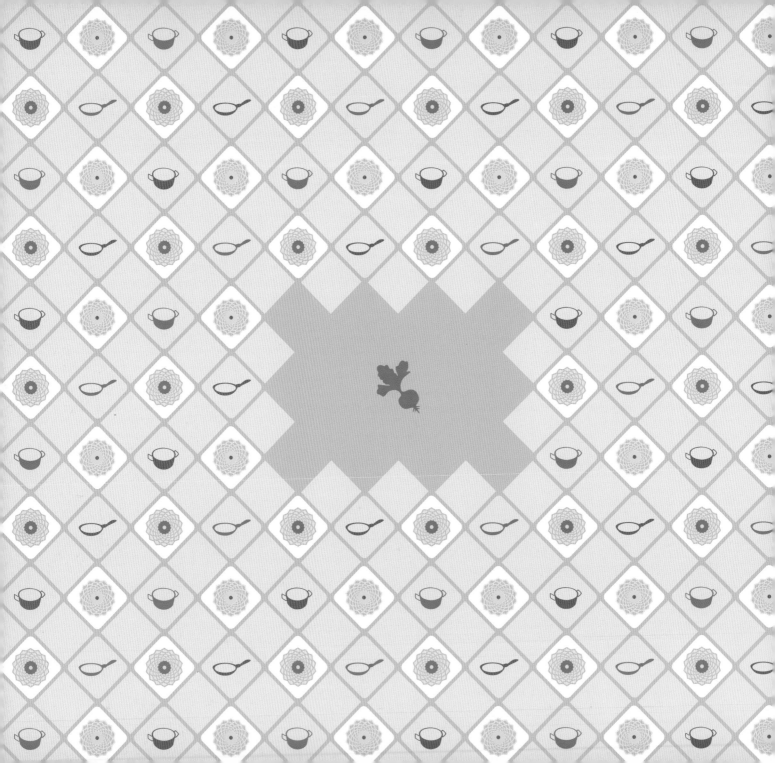

vegetarian

sweet pea, goat cheese, and watercress risotto

Risotto is the ultimate one-pot dish, and this recipe is a wonderful springtime variation that takes advantage of the season's bounty. Feel free to substitute other vegetables, depending on what's in season near you.

variation: Add cooked chicken or seafood to the risotto when you stir in the peas and goat cheese.

About 3 cups vegetable broth

10 ounces pearl onions, peeled, or 8 ounces frozen peeled pearl onions

2 tablespoons olive oil

½ cup finely chopped fennel

½ cup minced shallots

2 cloves garlic, minced

2 tablespoons minced fresh thyme

1 cup Arborio rice

½ cup dry white wine

1 bunch watercress, stemmed and chopped

1 cup fresh or frozen green peas

3 ounces soft goat cheese

½ cup (2 ounces) grated Parmesan cheese

Salt and freshly ground pepper to taste

SERVES 4

In a medium saucepan, bring the broth to a simmer over medium heat. Add the onions and cook for 5 minutes, or until slightly softened. Using a slotted spoon, transfer the onions to a small bowl. Keep the stock at a low simmer.

In a large, heavy skillet, heat the oil over medium heat. Add the fennel, shallots, garlic, and thyme. Cook for 3 to 5 minutes, or until softened. Add the rice and stir for 3 minutes, or until well coated. Add the wine and stir constantly until the wine is absorbed by the rice, 3 to 5 minutes.

Using a ladle, begin adding the broth ½ cup at a time. Keep stirring, letting the rice absorb all of the broth before you add more. After you have added 2 cups of the broth, add the watercress. Continue adding more broth, ½ cup at a time, until the rice is al dente, about 20 minutes total.

Stir in the peas, goat cheese, and Parmesan and stir for another 2 minutes to warm through. Season with salt and pepper.

To serve, scoop the risotto onto a large platter or divide among warmed bowls.

SMOKY MacaROnI anD CHeese

This version of macaroni and cheese is somewhat adult because of the smoki-
ness of the Cheddar cheese. For a more kid-friendly version, use mild Cheddar.
If you're the type who loves a crusty top on your mac 'n' cheese, use an ovenproof pot and brown it under the broiler just before serving. Once you see
how fast and easy it is to make this dish from scratch, you'll never reach for
a box again.

VaRIaTIon: For a more complete meal, just before serving, place a few handfuls of a seasonal vegetable, such as green beans, peas, broccoli, asparagus, or
cauliflower, in a steamer basket set in the pot or place the vegetable directly
on top of the macaroni and cheese. Cover and cook for 4 to 8 minutes, or until
crisp-tender.

1 pound macaroni or other dried
   shaped pasta
1 tablespoon olive oil
3 tablespoons unsalted butter
3 tablespoons all-purpose flour
3 cups whole milk

1 cup heavy cream or milk
¾ teaspoon dry mustard
¾ teaspoon sweet paprika
⅛ teaspoon ground nutmeg
2 cups (8 ounces) shredded aged
   Cheddar cheese

1 cup (4 ounces) shredded smoked
   Cheddar cheese
¾ cup (3 ounces) grated Asiago cheese
Salt and freshly ground white pepper
   to taste

SERVES 4 TO 6

In a large, heavy pot, cook the pasta in salted boiling water until al dente, 8 to
10 minutes. Drain the pasta in a colander and rinse under cold running water.
Transfer to a large bowl, toss with the olive oil, and set aside.

In the same pot, melt the butter over medium heat. Whisk in the flour and cook for 2 to 3 minutes, or until it bubbles. Combine the milk and cream and very gradually whisk it into the pot. Reduce the heat to low and add the mustard, paprika, and nutmeg, then the cheeses, one handful at a time, whisking constantly to make a smooth sauce.

Return the cooked pasta to pot and mix well with the sauce. Season with salt and pepper. Serve immediately, or if using an ovenproof pot, preheat the broiler and broil 4 to 6 inches from the heat source for 3 to 4 minutes, or until lightly browned and crisp.

To serve, put the pot on a trivet on the table with a large serving spoon alongside or serve in warmed shallow bowls.

EGYPTIAN TOMATO STEW WITH LENTILS AND MACARONI

This recipe was inspired by cooking with my friend David Smith. He lived for many years in Egypt, where this dish is available on almost every street corner in Cairo. Here, it is cooked in stages rather than using a multitude of pots, which is the more traditional way. The pasta and lentils are cooked together, then the remaining ingredients are added and cooked until the sauce is thickened. The heat of the sauce is enough to warm up the lentils and macaroni.

VARIATION: This is a vegetarian dish, but should you desire, cooked lamb, beef, or chicken could be added at the end.

8 ounces macaroni or other dried shaped
    pasta
1 cup green lentils
1 tablespoon dried oregano
3 tablespoons olive oil
Salt and freshly ground pepper to taste
1 yellow onion, chopped

3 cloves garlic, minced
1 tablespoon ground cumin
1 teaspoon ground coriander
1 teaspoon sweet paprika
One 6-ounce can tomato paste
4 cups finely chopped canned tomatoes
    (juices reserved)

2 tablespoons sugar
1 teaspoon red pepper flakes (optional)
½ cup finely chopped green onions,
    including green parts, for garnish

SERVES 4 TO 6

In a large, heavy pot, cook the pasta in salted boiling water until al dente, about 8 minutes. Using a slotted spoon, transfer the macaroni to a colander, reserving the pasta water in the pot for cooking the lentils. Rinse the macaroni under cold running water, then transfer to a large bowl. Add the oregano and 1 tablespoon olive oil. Toss well to coat. Set aside.

Add the lentils to the pot and bring to a boil. Reduce the heat to low, cover, and cook for 15 to 20 minutes, or until firm but tender. Drain the lentils, then add them to the bowl with the macaroni. Season with salt and pepper, toss well, and set aside.

≫ ≫ ≫ ≫

In the same pot over medium heat, heat the remaining 2 tablespoons olive oil. Add the yellow onion, garlic, cumin, coriander, and paprika and cook, stirring occasionally, for about 5 minutes, or until the onions are slightly softened.

Stir in the tomato paste, tomatoes and juice, and sugar, then season with salt and pepper to taste. Bring the sauce to a boil, then reduce the heat to low and simmer, uncovered, for about 30 minutes, or until thickened. If you want a spicy sauce, add the red pepper flakes.

Serve the lentils and macaroni at room temperature, with the piping hot tomato stew ladled over. Garnish with the green onions.

ZUCCHINI "NOODLES" WITH TOMATO SAUCE TO THE THIRD POWER

Thin slices of zucchini are a nutritious, low-carb substitute for pasta and are perfectly matched with this tomato sauce. They also make a wonderfully surprising, elegant-looking presentation. I jokingly refer to this sauce as taking tomatoes to the third power because the combination of fresh and sun-dried tomatoes creates a third stage of deeper flavor. The sauce is also awesome served over real noodles, which can be cooked in the same pot ahead of time.

variation: Add shrimp, scallops, or bite-sized pieces of any firm fish to the tomato sauce 10 minutes before it is finished cooking.

4 tablespoons extra-virgin olive oil
1 small onion, finely chopped
3 cloves garlic, minced
2 pounds very ripe fresh tomatoes, peeled and seeded (juices reserved)

¼ cup oil-packed sun-dried tomatoes, drained and chopped
¼ cup dry red wine
2 tablespoons minced fresh oregano
½ cup chopped fresh basil

Salt and freshly ground pepper to taste
1 pound yellow or green zucchini, cut into thin lengthwise slices with a vegetable peeler
2 tablespoons grated Parmesan cheese, or more to taste

SERVES 4

In a large pot, heat 3 tablespoons of the olive oil over medium heat. Add the onion and garlic and cook for 1 minute. Add the fresh tomatoes and juices, and the sun-dried tomatoes and simmer for 15 minutes, or until the sauce thickens slightly.

Add the red wine, oregano, and ¼ cup of the basil and season with salt and pepper. Simmer for 10 minutes to marry the flavors.

Just before serving, place the zucchini slices in a bowl. Sprinkle lightly with salt and pepper and toss with the remaining 1 tablespoon of olive oil. Place the slices in a steamer basket set in the pot or add them to the sauce. Cover and cook over medium-high heat for about 5 minutes, or until the slices are soft but still hold their shape.

Serve on a large platter or on warmed plates, sprinkled with the grated cheese and the remaining basil.

STEWED ROMANO BEANS WITH TOMATOES AND BASIL

Being of Italian lineage, I like some vegetables cooked until very soft. When Romano beans are in season, I always stew them. This is an almost no-fail dish, because the more the beans are stewed, the better they seem to become.

VARIATIONS: For a complete meal, put seasoned fish fillets, chicken, or spicy sausages on top of the beans when they're done and cook to the desired doneness. Or, serve on top of pasta, cooked in the same pot, of course.

2 to 3 tablespoons olive oil
1 large onion, coarsely chopped
½ large red bell pepper, seeded and coarsely chopped
2 to 3 cloves garlic, coarsely chopped
2 large tomatoes, seeded and coarsely chopped

1 cup water
Leaves from 5 or 6 oregano sprigs, chopped
1 small bunch basil, stemmed and coarsely chopped
1 pound green or yellow Romano beans, trimmed
2 tablespoons balsamic vinegar

2 tablespoons sugar
Salt and freshly ground pepper to taste
Grated Asiago cheese for garnish

SERVES 4 TO 6

In a large, heavy pot, heat the olive oil over medium heat. Add the onion, bell pepper, and garlic and cook for a few minutes, until slightly softened. Add the tomatoes, water, oregano, and half the basil. Cover and simmer for about 30 minutes, or until slightly thickened.

Add the beans and simmer over low heat for about 30 minutes, or until soft. Add the remaining basil, the vinegar, sugar, salt, and pepper.

Turn off the heat and let the stew sit for 15 minutes before serving in warmed bowls, sprinkled with grated cheese.

any-season vegetable stir-fry with orange, ginger, and lemongrass

A wok is a wonderful one-pot vessel. The most important part of wok cooking is knowing how long it takes to cook each ingredient. Some foods, like meat or poultry, are lightly cooked, then removed from the wok to be returned later when the dish is finished. Dense vegetables like beets, carrots, and winter squash are added before more tender vegetables like zucchini, asparagus, and green beans, which require only a few minutes. The orange, ginger, and lemongrass in this recipe will complement any vegetables you choose. If you don't have a wok, use a large skillet.

serving suggestions: To serve as a complete meal, add tofu, tempeh, or seitan and serve over steamed rice.

1 tablespoon grated orange zest
1/3 cup fresh orange juice
2 tablespoons soy sauce
1 heaping teaspoon cornstarch
2 tablespoons minced fresh ginger
3 tablespoons minced fresh cilantro

1 tablespoon vegetable oil
1 or 2 stalks lemongrass, white parts only, peeled and minced
2 leeks, white parts only, washed and cut into ½-inch-thick slices
1 clove garlic, minced

One 6-ounce can water chestnuts, drained
½ to 1 teaspoon red pepper flakes (optional)
3 cups chopped or sliced seasonal vegetables
Salt and freshly ground pepper to taste

SERVES 4 TO 6

In a small bowl, whisk together the orange zest, orange juice, soy sauce, cornstarch, ginger, and cilantro.

In a wok, heat the oil over medium-high heat. Add the lemongrass, leeks, garlic, and water chestnuts and stir-fry for 2 to 3 minutes. If you want a spicy stir-fry, add the red pepper flakes at this time.

Begin adding the seasonal vegetables, in descending order of their density. Add a little water, cover, and cook the dense vegetables until crisp-tender. Uncover and add the remaining vegetables and stir-fry until crisp-tender. If the vegetables require longer cooking times, lower the heat and cover for a few minutes.

Add the orange juice mixture. Cook and stir for 5 minutes, or until the juices turn clear and thicken slightly. Adjust the seasoning to your taste.

To serve, use tongs to transfer to a platter or warmed plates.

SHIITAKE AND VEGETABLE STEW WITH SEITAN

Seitan, made from wheat gluten, is a wonderful source of protein that makes this dish a complete meal. It's often referred to as "mock" chicken or beef in vegetarian Chinese cooking. You will find it in most natural foods stores, usually near the tofu or tempeh, or in many Asian markets under the name Mi-Tan. If you can find seitan seasoned with herbs or even smoked, it would be great in this recipe.

Once you gather the ingredients, this stew comes together quickly. It also freezes well, so consider doubling the recipe.

SERVING SUGGESTION: A spinach salad with a sesame dressing would be a great complement to this one-pot meal.

2 tablespoons olive oil

1 onion, coarsely chopped

1 stalk celery, thinly sliced

1 carrot, peeled and thinly sliced

½ large red bell pepper, seeded and thinly sliced

6 ounces shiitake mushrooms, stemmed and sliced

2 tablespoons cream sherry

Salt and freshly ground pepper to taste

2 tablespoons unsalted butter, or olive oil for a vegan stew

2 tablespoons minced fresh thyme

2 cloves garlic, minced

¼ cup all-purpose flour

3 cups vegetable broth

8 to 10 ounces seitan, cut into 1-inch cubes

²/₃ cup fresh or frozen green peas

²/₃ cup fresh or frozen corn kernels

SERVES 4 TO 6 GENEROUSLY

In a large, heavy pot, heat the olive oil over medium heat. Add the onion, celery, carrot, and bell pepper. Cook for about 5 minutes, or until the vegetables are slightly softened. Add the mushrooms and sherry and cook for another 5 minutes to soften them. Season with salt and pepper. Transfer all the ingredients and juices to a large bowl.

In the same pot, melt the butter or heat the olive oil over medium heat. Add the thyme and garlic and cook for 2 minutes. Whisk in the flour and cook for 2 minutes, stirring constantly, or until it bubbles. Gradually whisk in the broth and cook for another 5 minutes, or until the sauce thickens slightly. Return the cooked vegetables along with the seitan, peas, and corn to the pot. Cook for 1 minute to heat through.

To serve, spoon into warmed shallow bowls.

WHOLE GRAINS WITH CAULIFLOWER, OLIVES, AND FETA

I can make an entire meal out of savory whole grains. I first made this dish with sorghum, an ancient grain used in African cooking, though other whole grains can be substituted.

VARIATION: When artichokes are in season, look for small ones at farmers' markets or local grocers and add them to this dish along with, or in place of, the cauliflower. Trim the tops and remove the outer leaves. The choke hasn't developed and doesn't need to be removed.

3 cups water
1 cup whole grains, such as sorghum, wheat berries, or barley
2 cups small cauliflower florets
¼ cup minced fresh oregano
2 green onions, including green parts, finely chopped

¼ cup extra-virgin olive oil, plus more for dipping
1 tablespoon grated lemon zest
3 tablespoons fresh lemon juice
½ cup pitted kalamata olives
¼ cup pine nuts, toasted
Salt and freshly ground pepper to taste

1 cup (5 ounces) crumbled feta cheese
Pinch of cayenne pepper
6 to 8 warmed pita breads

SERVES 4

In a large pot, bring the water to a boil and add the whole grains. Reduce heat to low and simmer for 30 to 40 minutes, or until the grains are tender.

Add the cauliflower, oregano, onions, the ¼ cup olive oil, the lemon zest and juice, olives, pine nuts, salt, and pepper. Cover and cook for 5 to 7 minutes, or until the cauliflower is soft.

Add the feta and season with cayenne. Stir well and remove from the heat. Cover and let stand for 5 minutes to warm the feta. Taste and adjust the seasoning.

Serve in warmed bowls, with pita breads and olive oil for dipping.

egg foo yung

This classic Chinese one-pot egg dish is something I make often. I just love the combination of crunchy vegetables with silky scrambled eggs. I use canned straw mushrooms, readily found in most grocery stores in the Asian food section, but fresh mushrooms would be a great substitute.

This dish keeps well in the refrigerator and is good either warm or at room temperature. Using a nonstick sauté pan makes it easier to unmold onto a platter.

variation: When sautéing the cabbage, add seitan, tofu, or tempeh.

10 large eggs

3 to 4 tablespoons soy sauce

½ cup minced fresh cilantro

1 teaspoon Tabasco sauce (optional)

5 tablespoons vegetable oil

1 onion, thinly sliced

2 cups finely shredded cabbage

One 6-ounce can straw mushrooms, drained, or 6 ounces fresh button or stemmed shiitake mushrooms

4 ounces bean sprouts

Salt and freshly ground pepper to taste

SERVES 4 TO 6

In a medium bowl, whisk the eggs, soy sauce, cilantro, and optional Tabasco together. Set aside.

In a large, heavy nonstick skillet, heat 2 ½ tablespoons of the oil over medium heat. Add the onion and cabbage and cook for 5 minutes, or until soft. Add the mushrooms and sprouts and cook for another 2 minutes, or until the sprouts just begin to soften. Season lightly with salt and pepper.

≫ ≫ ≫ ≫

Add the remaining 2 ½ tablespoons oil to the pan and stir. Pour the egg mixture over the vegetables and reduce the heat to low. Using a spatula, gently lift the edges of the egg and let the liquid run under the solid eggs until most of the egg is cooked. Cover and cook for about 5 minutes, or until the cake is lightly browned on the bottom.

Remove from the heat and let sit for 2 minutes. Using a spatula, loosen the outer edges and shake the pan to loosen the cake. Put a large plate on top of the pan and carefully invert both.

To serve, cut into 6 to 8 wedges and serve on warmed plates.

SPICE COAST VEGETABLE CURRY

Vegetable curries are irresistible, and there is nothing like creating your own curry blend. As my buddy Stuart Dickson, farmer and cook extraordinaire, taught me, once you have purchased all the spices needed, you will use them all the time. It's best to buy spices in relatively small batches at Indian or other ethnic markets, where turnover is high and they are guaranteed to be fresh. Supermarket jarred offerings pale in comparison.

This particular curry blend has a deep, earthy flavor with an enticing aroma. This dish is sensational served fresh from the pot, but it will be just as good, if not better, the next day.

SERVING SUGGESTION: Serve over steamed rice prepared in the pot before, or after, the curry.

2 tablespoons vegetable oil
1 tablespoon mustard seeds
1 tablespoon ground coriander
1 tablespoon ground cumin
¼ to ½ teaspoon cayenne pepper
½ teaspoon freshly ground pepper
2 teaspoons ground turmeric
1 teaspoon ground fennel seed

2 teaspoons ground cinnamon
½ teaspoon ground cloves
1 onion, finely chopped
2 potatoes, peeled and cut into 1-inch cubes
2 carrots, peeled and sliced into ½-inch-thick rounds
1 red Thai or jalapeño chili, seeded and coarsely chopped

¼ cup minced fresh ginger
1½ cups vegetable broth
1½ cups coconut milk
1½ cups cauliflower florets
½ cup fresh or frozen green peas
Salt and freshly ground pepper to taste

SERVES 6 OR MORE

In a large, heavy pot, heat the oil over medium heat. Add the mustard seeds and toast for 1 minute, or until they sputter and pop. Add the coriander, cumin, cayenne, pepper, turmeric, fennel, cinnamon, and cloves, then stir in the onion and cook for 3 minutes to bring out the oils in the spices.

» » » »

Add the potatoes, carrots, chili, ginger, and broth. Bring to a boil, then reduce the heat to low, cover, and simmer, stirring occasionally, for 30 minutes, or until the potatoes and carrots are soft.

Add the coconut milk, cauliflower, and peas and simmer for 5 to 7 minutes, or until all the ingredients are tender. Season with salt and pepper.

To serve, ladle into warmed bowls.

index

TABLE OF EQUIVALENTS

The exact equivalents in the following tables have been rounded for convenience.

LIQUID/DRY MEASURES

U.S.	Metric
¼ teaspoon	1.25 milliliters
½ teaspoon	2.5 milliliters
1 teaspoon	5 milliliters
1 tablespoon (3 teaspoons)	15 milliliters
1 fluid ounce (2 tablespoons)	30 milliliters
¼ cup	60 milliliters
⅓ cup	80 milliliters
½ cup	120 milliliters
1 cup	240 milliliters
1 pint (2 cups)	480 milliliters
1 quart (4 cups; 32 ounces)	960 milliliters
1 gallon (4 quarts)	3.84 liters
1 ounce (by weight)	28 grams
1 pound	454 grams
2.2 pounds	1 kilogram

LENGTH

U.S.	Metric
⅛ inch	3 millimeters
¼ inch	6 millimeters
½ inch	12 millimeters
1 inch	2.5 centimeters

OVEN TEMPERATURE

Fahrenheit	Celsius	Gas
250	120	½
275	140	1
300	150	2
325	160	3
350	180	4
375	190	5
400	200	6
425	220	7
450	230	8
475	240	9
500	260	10